T0154362

NUTS

To

Jane: Mat and Tabitha
Sally: Mum and Magic
With all our love

THE ENGLISH KITCHEN

NUTS
GROWING AND COOKING

JANE MCMORLAND HUNTER

AND

SALLY HUGHES

PROSPECT BOOKS

2017

This edition published in 2017 in Great Britain and the USA by Prospect Books at 26 Parke Road, London, SW13 9NG

© 2017, Jane McMorland Hunter and Sally Hughes
© 2017, illustrations, Sally Hughes

The authors assert their right to be identified as the authors in accordance with the Copyright, Designs & Patents Act 1988.

British Library Cataloguing in Publication Data:
A catalogue entry for this book is available from the British Library.

No part of this publication may be reproduced, stored in a retrieval system or transmitted in any form or by any means, electronic, mechanical, photocopying, recording or otherwise, without the prior permission of the copyright holders.

ISBN 13: 978-1-909248-54-0

Printed by the Gutenberg Press Ltd., Malta.

TABLE OF CONTENTS

INTRODUCTION

Nuts are part of our everyday life and language. A tricky problem is 'a hard nut to crack', a well-put argument captures the situation 'in a nutshell', people 'go nuts' or use a 'sledgehammer to crack a nut'. Bowls of salty peanuts are a traditional accompaniment to a drink, marrons glacés are a delightful indulgence and a sprinkle of chopped nuts provides the finishing touch to a knickerbocker glory. Nuts are an essential ingredient in every cuisine from the delicately scented pilau and rich spicy groundnut stew to the Bakewell tart and hazelnut meringue.

Nuts have noble origins. Hazels have been grown in Britain since prehistoric times and were believed to ward off evil. Almonds were regarded as a sign of resurrection in Biblical lands, with sugared almonds ensuring good luck at New Year. Since Roman times, walnuts, the most noble of all nuts, have been thrown at wedding ceremonies as symbols of fertility and used to cure all manner of ills. Land was measured by how much mast it produced and right up to the First World War, English school children were given a day off on Holy Cross day in September in order to go nutting.

Nuts feature in literature from Beatrix Potter's *Tales* and the popular and often allegorical nursery rhymes *I had a little nut tree* and *Here we go gathering nuts in May* to Jon Stallworthy's heart-wrenching poem *The Almond Tree*. And who doesn't enjoy singing along to Burl Ives and Johnny Cash's rendition of that classic American civil war song *Eatin' Goober Peas?* Whether as food, medicine, myth or entertainment, nuts have always been an important part of our lives.

They are a nutritious food source, enjoyed by Native Americans, Aborigines and foragers worldwide. They are also treats: sticky rose-scented baklava, chewy almond nougat and bags of sizzling, hot chestnuts brought from a street stall at Christmas. Today, a new generation of cooks are turning to nuts to help adapt their favourite recipes for friends with dairy and gluten allergies.

From a simple handful of scroggin (trail mix) to a sophisticated nut cheesecake, nuts can deliver something delicious, however much or little time you have available. We have included over seventy recipes from a spiced pecan and pumpkin salad to a crowd-pleasing walnut cake or a Christmas nut loaf to a Norwegian birthday spectacular. We have also provided storage and handling tips, and ways to make your own nut products such as nut milks and nut butters.

Healthwise, nuts are not so much a super as a wonder food. Part of the human diet for centuries, they are easy to store and transport and are one of the most concentrated foods available, packing a tremendous amount into a tiny, but delectable package. True, a small proportion of the population has a nut allergy, but for the majority of us nuts are a tremendous source of key vitamins and nutrients, and nut consumption has been associated with a reduced risk of heart disease. We look at the health benefits of the different nut varieties and ways to incorporate them into a healthy diet.

Traditionally, nut trees are planted for future generations but this book shows how you can have a harvest within a season, even in a small space. Hazels, almonds and even the more unusual pistachios and peanuts are within the reach of most gardeners. So whether you are planning a whole nuttery or a little nut tree in a container, read on. We have even given thought to those creatures that share our gardens and included information on fat balls and bird tables.

A strict botanical definition of nuts is tricky, excluding as it does peanuts and pistachios. However we feel that if cooks and gardeners think of something as a nut so will we, so we are including the full range you would find in your local health food store or park, from Brazils to pecans, hazels to acorns. Where it tastes good we have included recipes and if you can grow it or forage for it in Britain or the temperate United States or Europe, we have provided planting and hunting advice.

THE STORY OF NUTS

A story is like the wind, it comes from a far off place.

(Laurens van der Post, *A Story Like the Wind*)

The story of nuts is one of ancient histories, exotic places, improbable promises and delectable feasts.

Long before the development of agriculture, man depended entirely on foods he could hunt or gather. Nuts grew wild in most regions of the world, were easy to store, and were highly nutritious; it is hardly surprising that they were such an important food. They are one of the oldest food plants and appeared at the end of the Cretaceous Period, just as the dinosaurs began to decline. This was over sixty million years ago, before North America and Europe split into two separate continents, so indigenous species of walnuts, hazelnuts and chestnuts exist on both sides of the Atlantic. During the cold of the Ice Ages, many died out but re-emerged in North America and Asia with the advancing warmth.

A great many nuts have their present origins in the near east and central Asia and came to Europe via Greece. They thrived on the lower slopes of the Caucasus Mountains where even today there are entire woods of walnut trees and mountain valleys filled with almonds.

Celtic tribes arrived in Britain in 700 BC and evidence from pollen shows that they began cultivating nut trees, probably choosing the most productive, hazels. The Romans are credited with bringing almonds, sweet chestnuts and possibly walnuts to Britain. They may have complained about the weather and introduced the dubious concept of wearing socks with sandals but they recognised that our fertile soil and temperate climate suited a wide range of plants.

When the Roman Empire collapsed, much of Europe reverted to the ways of life they had known previously. Britain entered the Dark Ages and, all over Western Europe, farming methods became less sophisticated. Simpler crops were grown, fruit trees were left untended and many people relied on harvests they could gather, rather than cultivate. The exceptions were the monasteries. Monastic gardens were places of both productivity and contemplation, and nuts were a vital part of these gardens. A plan from about 820 AD survives for the Benedictine Monastery of St. Gall in Switzerland. As in many monastery gardens, the orchard was also a burial ground and there is evidence of specialized areas for almonds, hazels, walnuts and chestnuts, as well as fruit trees. Monasteries like this would have existed in Britain, ensuring that the cultivation of nut trees continued.

The Tudor reign marked the beginning of a period of relative stability, which enabled the people of Britain to contemplate gardening in a long-term light. In order to consider planting trees, a householder, whether rich or poor, needs to be reasonably certain that he or his descendants will be around to see the fruits of his labours. Increasingly people felt they were safe to plan ahead, with the rich planting avenues, orchards and specimen trees and the less well-off planting hazels from which they could harvest wood in five to ten years. At much the same time in America, settlers had a hard life but they too planned for the future and planted trees. After all, they had travelled thousands of miles in search of new and stable homes where they could put down roots and establish themselves.

In the nineteenth century, agricultural cultivation programmes were extended to include nuts and new, commercial cultivars were developed around the world. Today, there are plantations of nut trees from California to India and even in Kent the once-declining hazel plats are now, slowly, increasing.

Nuts also have strong links with magic and myth. In Mediterranean countries, nuts are often given as wedding gifts or, perhaps more riskily, thrown at the newly-married couple. These ceremonies date back to ancient times when nuts were regarded as symbols of fertility and hope.

Nutcrack Night is another name for All Hallows' Eve or Hallowe'en. For the villagers in Oliver Goldsmith's *The Vicar of Wakefield,* the tradition of burning nuts and playing tricks was every bit as important as singing Christmas carols or eating pancakes on Shrove Tuesday.

'Here we go gathering nuts in May' may seem a strange idea as there are no nuts to harvest in May, unless perhaps in Australia, but this is a very British rhyme. What has actually happened is that 'nuts' is a corruption of 'knots', which refers to the knots or bunches of flowers which were traditionally gathered on May Day.

Another traditional nursery rhyme featuring nuts is about the improbable little nut tree which will bear nothing but a silver nutmeg and a golden pear. Again the rhyme is not about nuts, but King Henry VII's attempts to secure a satisfactory marriage for his heir with the royal family of Spain. In this case, the nut tree was probably England and the 'fruits' the wealth that would benefit both countries.

In days gone by, harvesting nuts, or nutting as it was called, was often associated with debauched behaviour. It was a jolly affair with the womenfolk of the village harvesting for food or dyes. The whole village would join them, with the men sneaking off from the fields for a little illicit behaviour in the shelter of the copses. Richard Mabey in *Flora Britannica* recounts the story of the owner of Hatfield Forest in Essex who, in 1826, complained:

> as soon as the Nuts begin to get ripe...the idle and disorderly Men and Women of bad Character from [Bishop's] Stortford... come... in large parties to gather the Nuts or under pretence of gathering Nuts to loiter about in Crowds....and in the Evening....take Beer and Spirits and Drink into the Forest

which affords them an opportunity for all sorts of Debauchery.

Up until the First World War, many schools closed on All Hallows' Eve and families would make it a day out. Some places held to the belief that if you went nutting on a holy day, you would meet the Devil although others used Holy Cross or Holy Rood Day on 14 September to mark the start of the harvest. This was the day when St. Helena claimed to have discovered Christ's Cross. In Roman times, Jews were compelled to listen to a sermon in a Christian church and during the Middle Ages it became a feast day, gradually becoming a seasonal celebration rather than a religious one.

Nuts appear frequently in literature, with Beatrix Potter writing stories about both red and grey squirrels and their hoards of nuts. Squirrel Nutkin is a cheeky red squirrel, who takes his name from the female flowers of the hazel, while *The Tale of Timmy Tiptoes* tells the story of a chubby grey squirrel and was written especially for the American market. Cicely Mary Barker's *Flower Fairies* poems include almost all the nut trees, with hazel catkins and almond blossom heralding the arrival of spring, and hazelnuts and beechnuts announcing autumn. The outlaws in B.B.'s (Denys Watkins-Pitchford) *Brendon Chase* largely survive on nuts for a time saying:

Nuts are like chocolates, you can go on eating them until you feel you never want to see another.

Until, of course, the next day.

ALMONDS

There are two types of almonds; the edible or sweet almonds (*Prunus dulcis*) and bitter almonds (*P. dulcis* var. *amara*). The bitter nuts are poisonous as they produce prussic acid or hydrogen cyanide when mixed with water. Alexandre Dumas' warning is clear enough: 'The most rapid and violent of poisons'. Once heated, the bitter nuts become harmless and their oil is widely used in the cosmetics and medical industries and can be used for cooking. They contain the strong 'almondy' flavour found in almond extract, which is absent in sweet almonds. It is used in some marzipans, Amaretto liqueur, Amaretti biscuits and other dishes where a strong almond flavour is required. In Sicily, the trees are said to be like love: bitter and sweet. It is believed the nuts can only be distinguished when the trees are flowering; the redder the flowers the more bitter the nuts.

Almonds originally come from the Middle East and Central Asia, spreading along the Silk Road to the Mediterranean. They have been found amongst Neolithic remains at Knossos on Crete (dating from about 8,000 BC) and by the Bronze Age (c 3,000 BC), they had been domesticated. Thirty almonds were found in the tomb of Tutankhamun, buried in 1,323 BC. They grew wild in Palestine and are frequently mentioned in the Bible; Aaron's rod which bore flowers and fruit at the same time was almond wood and the nuts were included among the presents that were taken to Egypt by the sons of Jacob. The Romans called them Greek nuts and brought them to Britain in the first century AD but probably as imported nuts rather than trees. By the Middle Ages, they were established as an important crop in Southern Europe and the warmer regions of Britain. John Gerard noted in his *Great Herball* of 1578: 'The naturall place of the Almond is in the hot regions, yet we have them in our London gardens and orchards in great plenty.' They reached California in the mid eighteenth century and this is where most are now grown, followed by Italy and Spain.

They were important as almond milk could replace cow's milk on the many traditional fast days. They were also eaten as a snack; green nuts were sold in bags with a packet of salt to dip them in. Part of their popularity stemmed from the fact that they were believed to prevent drunkenness. The Ancient Greeks and Romans believed bitter almonds prevented one from getting drunk but as by eating these nuts you also ran the risk of poisoning yourself this was a fine example of 'choose your poison'.

The trees blossom very early in the year and, because of this, they are often regarded as symbols of optimism. In the Bible, they represent the Resurrection and in Victorian flower language they mean hope. Sugared almonds are traditional presents at weddings and christenings and if given at New Year they ensure a sweet year for the recipient. In Greece the trees are called *phylla,* after Phyllis, a Thracian princess. In Greek mythology she is jilted at the altar and kills herself. The goddess Athena transforms her into an almond tree which stands over her grave. When her true lover finds her grave and embraces the tree, it bursts into flower. In Jon Stallworthy's autobiographical poem about the birth of his son the tree offers hope and then, when hope is lost, it mirrors the change in the father's life:

> Only when
> the buds, all the buds, were broken
> would the tree be in full sail.

Historically almonds were the nut of choice in the kitchen. The Romans used them in stuffings, cakes and even omelettes. Ground almonds were used as a thickener and from medieval times onwards the Middle Eastern invention marchpane, or marzipan, was used as the base for the spectacular sculptures which graced the tables at feasts and festivals. Harold McGee recounts the tale of a cross Leonardo da Vinci who made marzipan sculptures for the Milanese court in 1470. He 'observed with pain that [they] gobble up all the sculptures I give them, right to the last morsel'. Early cookbooks all have a high proportion of recipes for almonds. Household accounts dating from 1265 show that a family spent 12/6 (roughly 62½p) on 60 lbs (27 kg) of almonds but only 12d (5p) on shoes for Petronella the laundress. Nicholas Culpeper in his *Complete Herbal* of 1653 recommends a 'butter' of almonds, sugar and rosewater, to be eaten with violets, describing it as 'very wholesome and commodious for students for it rejoiceth the heart and comforteth the brain'. John Gerard has equal praise for the nut:

> The oyle which is newly pressed out of the sweet Almonds is a mitigater of paine and all manner of aches [...] The oile of Almonds makes smooth the hands and face of delicate persons, and clenseth the skin from all spots, pimples, and lentils.'

One wonders though what it would do for rougher persons.

Robert May's *The Accomplisht Cook* from 1685 included boiled puddings, custards, tarts, cakes, breads, biscuits and, of course, marchpane, the forerunner of marzipan. John Nott's *Cooks and Confectioners Dictionary* of 1723 had twenty-one recipes, expanding the range with almond cheese, cream, milk and puffs. The only other nuts he mentioned in detail were walnuts, with a mere five recipes. Just over a century later in 1861 Mrs Beeton added soup and cheesecakes to the repertoire. In 1925 Mrs C. F. Leyel wrote in *The Gentle Art of Cookery:* 'The possibilities of almonds are varied; they can be used to change a commonplace dish into a delicacy.'

BEECH MAST

We do not now consider beech mast a particularly vital crop but historically it was of great importance. The tree's Latin name *Fagus* comes from the Greek 'to eat' and the word 'mast' means 'food', although in both cases this probably referred to the diet of pigs, rather than humans. Prehistoric man, and the poor for many years later, ground the nuts into a meal, which was nourishing, if rather uninspiring. Beech mast has tended to be used as human food in times of shortage or famine, although John Gerard recommends it for kidney pain in his *Herball*. Native Americans and settlers both ate the nuts, and 'coffee' made from beech mast is an acceptable substitute if one is desperate. The oil produced from the nuts is a good alternative to olive oil, but it is not widely produced as the nuts are time-consuming to pick.

For many years, the value of land in Britain was frequently determined by the amount of mast (beech and acorns) it produced rather than the actual size. Thomas Tusser began life as a farmer but was never particularly successful and later turned his attention to poetry, writing the first, and probably only, rhyming farming manual. In 1573 he published his *Five Hundred Points of Good Husbandry,* expanded from the hundred-point version published sixteen years earlier. His advice on collecting mast is as follows:

To gather some mast, it shall stand thee upon,
with servant and children, er mast be all gon:
Some left among bushes shal pleasure thy swine,
for feare of a mischief keepe acrons fro kine*.

(*Kine: cows, for whom acorns are harmful)

The trees themselves are very beautiful, as Gilbert White of Selborne noted, describing them as 'the most lovely of all forest trees, whether we consider its smooth rind or bark, its glossy foliage, or graceful pendulous boughs'. Burnham Beeches in Buckinghamshire is the largest collection of beech trees in the world, with some of the pollarded trees being over five hundred years old. Only twenty miles outside London, in 1880 it was brought under the protection of the Corporation of the City of London. The poet Thomas Gray wrote his *Elegy Written in a Country Churchyard* less than half a mile from the wood and describes the trees, while in George Orwell's *Keep the Aspidistra Flying*, Gordon and Rosemary go there for the day and come to the conclusion that beeches look more like sentient creatures than other trees. She describes the fallen leaves as looking like gold, he as the colour of tomato soup; both are correct and the colours make walking through the woods on an autumn day one of life's great pleasures.

BRAZIL NUTS

Most Brazil nuts come from trees growing wild in the Amazon rain forest. Reaching 45 m / 150 feet tall, they are the largest trees in the forest with straight, thick trunks and huge glossy green leaves that spread above the canopy of smaller trees. The nuts are encased in a large capsule or pod, which can contain up to twenty-four nuts neatly arranged like the segments of an orange.

The Spanish first saw the nuts in the sixteenth century and called them the 'almonds of the Andes'. In 1836 they were imported to Britain where they immediately earned the title 'king of nuts'. Despite their popularity, attempts to cultivate Brazils outside the rain forest area have failed completely. Even within the Amazon Basin attempts have largely been unsuccessful, partly because the trees take twelve to fifteen years to fruit; meaning that a plantation is unlikely to show a profit within a practical period.

In the wild, the trees have developed a unique relationship with the agouti, a small rodent which eats Brazil nuts. During the harvest season they bury nuts 'for later', frequently forgetting where they have hidden their supplies. After twelve to eighteen months in the ground these forgotten nuts begin to grow into the future forest giants.

When ripe the pods, which can weigh up to 2 kilos, crash to the ground, making harvesting a risky business. For this reason harvesting is not usually carried out on windy days and the gatherers wear wide-brimmed wooden hats or carry shields.

The trees are now protected and cannot be felled, resulting in many isolated trees surrounded by houses or farmland. The problem is that the trees need a healthy rain forest to survive and, in cleared areas, there are no agoutis to spread the seed and safeguard the future of the trees.

CASHEWS

Cashew nuts may seem ordinary when one opens a packet but they grow in an extraordinary manner, each nut hanging from the base of a cashew 'apple'.

The trees are indigenous to Brazil but now grow throughout the Tropics and East Africa. They were probably discovered by Portuguese explorers, who gave us the name cashew, mishearing the Brazilian name *acaju* as caju. The trees are tolerant of a wide range of soils and were planted in coastal regions of India and Mozambique, at first to prevent soil erosion rather than for their harvest.

The evergreen trees have tough leathery leaves and can reach up to 12 m / 40 feet but are usually considerably smaller. As the flowers fade bright yellow or orange pear-shaped fruits develop. At the base of these grow the cashew nuts, encased within a double shell. Between the two shells is toxic oil which can burn the skin unpleasantly, giving the nuts their Brazilian name which means 'to pucker the mouth'. Heat destroys the oil so cashews are usually roasted whole before the kernel is extracted.

The cashew apples are also edible but they do not keep well, lasting little more than a day. In Goa they are trampled by foot and used to make kaju feni, the local liquor, but can also be made into jams and chutneys, or dried and candied.

SWEET CHESTNUTS

Sweet chestnuts originated in Central Asia but these trees spread across the globe many millions of years ago, and fossilized remains have been discovered in several locations, placing them in prehistoric Europe, Greenland and Alaska. They were then driven out by the advancing cold of the Ice Age. The Greeks brought the cultivated trees back to Europe and the Romans then took them through France to Britain.

Their Latin name (*Castanea*) was thought to come from Kastania, a town in Thessaly, Greece but it is more likely that the town was named after the Latin or Greek name for the trees, which grew particularly well in the area. Henry David Thoreau has a delightful explanation for the common English name: 'Chestnut – evidently because it is packed in a little chest.'

American chestnuts (*C. dentata*) sustained the pioneer settlers with both wood for their homes and nuts. A few trees were always left near the homesteads for their autumn harvest. Almost all these trees were destroyed by chestnut blight. It was discovered in New York City Zoological Park in 1904 and was thought to have been introduced on imported chestnuts from Asia. It was carried by birds, insects and wind and spread rapidly, destroying an estimated 9 million acres of chestnut forest.

The Great Chestnut of Tortworth in Gloucestershire was chosen by the Tree Council as one of fifty great British trees in 2002 to commemorate the Queen's Golden Jubilee. It was at least a hundred years old when it was listed as a boundary marker in King John's reign (1199-1216). Legend has it that the tree grew from a nut planted during King Egbert's reign in 800. The tree has been allowed to spread outwards and now forms a copse of its own with a plaque from 1800:

May Man still Guard thy Venerable form
From the Rude Blasts and Tempestuous Storm.
Still may thou Flourish through Succeeding time,
And Last, long Last, the Wonder of the Clime.

Wild chestnuts are often called the bread tree or the tree of bread due to their ability to sustain people. At various times they have formed the staple diet in Italy, Spain, Corsica and Turkey, particularly in mountainous regions where cereals will not grow. In Britain fasting means bread and water, in France it refers to chestnuts and water. They could be eaten fresh or roasted and ground chestnuts could be used to thicken soup and porridge as well as made into bread.

Virgil and Pliny both mention chestnuts and Apicius has a recipe for boiled lentils with a highly seasoned chestnut sauce. Boiled chestnuts with Brussels sprouts was apparently Goethe's favourite dish. Edward Bunyard recommends: 'I think the Chestnut finds its best end within a bird of some sort – and preferably a dead bird.'

In France and Italy, sweet chestnuts are divided into *marrons* with a single large nut and *châtaignes* with 2-5 kernels. *Châtaignes* are said to be the food of the poor while *marrons* are reputed to be sweeter, with a better flavour and are used to make luxuries such as marrons glacés and chestnut purée. Candied chestnuts became popular in southern France and northern Italy when the Crusaders returned with sugar, but it was not until the seventeenth century that the nuts gained the final glaze that distinguishes a true marron glacé. France and Italy both claim the credit for this final refinement.

Another famous dessert, the Mont-Blanc, also has disputed origins. The Angelina Café in Paris claims its invention in 1903 and still serves the delightfully indulgent concoction of meringue, cream and chestnut paste vermicelli piled up to resemble the mountain. A similar dessert was described in an Italian cookbook of 1475 and possibly served to Lucrezia Borgia, perhaps a less desirable claim.

Chestnuts are regarded as an aphrodisiac in China and Arabia and John Evelyn said that the leaves could be used as a mattress, although he did admit that they made a 'crackling noise'. According to Culpeper's seventeenth-century herbal the nuts could be used to abort pregnancy or cure coughs. The leaves were used by the Crusaders to relieve burns, a necessary relief from the popular weapon of boiling tar which was poured down from castle battlements. Last but not least, the wood is used, among other things, to make castanets.

HAZELNUTS

Hazels grew in Britain long before it was separated from Continental Europe in prehistoric times. After the Ice Age, they were one of the first trees to grow on the newly emerging land. As the larger oaks and ashes grew, the hazels moved to the edges of woodlands and became the hedgerow plants we know today.

The name hazel comes from the Anglo-Saxon *haesel* meaning hat or cap, from the frilly husks. *Corylus,* the Latin genus, comes from the Greek *korys* or helmet, also referring to the husk. Cultivation began in Classical times and the species name *avellana* probably comes from Abellina, the old name for the valley round Damascus in Syria. It referred to the trees imported to Greece for cultivation as opposed to the wild ones already growing in the countryside and was mentioned by Pliny, who also had the warning 'filberts put more fat on the body than one would think at all likely'.

In the seventeenth century, Avellino in Campagnia, Italy became a centre for hazel growing and the trees now grow wild in the valleys there. Alexandre Dumas in his *Le Grand Dictionnaire de Cuisine* tells the story of how Victor Hugo nearly fell to his death while picking nuts in these valleys as a boy.

The trees divide into two main types: cobs and filberts, with a confusing amount of overlap. In 1597 John Gerard described the cobnut as 'our hedge nut or hassel nut tree' and the filbert as 'that which groweth in gardens and orchards'.

The name cob probably comes for the Old English *cop* meaning head, again referring to the frilly caps the nuts wear. In medieval times 'to cob' meant to throw gently and two games seem to have developed based on the nuts. Coblenut was a game played by sixteenth-century children, thought to be similar to conkers. In Cobnut small nuts were placed in piles and the players took it in turns to try to knock them down with larger nuts. Any nuts they dislodged became theirs, the player with the most nuts at the end winning. Like so many names associated with hazels, the two frequently appear interchangeable.

Filberts were called 'full-beards', describing the frilly husk which covers the entire nut. Later, when it was realised that the trees needed to be separated from their magical and pagan heritage (hazels were associated with witches and druid ceremonies were frequently held in hazel groves) they became known as filberts, a corruption of Philibert. This seventh-century Saint's Day falls on 20 August, conveniently close to the start of the nutting season.

Historically filberts were more highly prized than the native cobs. John Parkinson describes them as 'the best kinde of Hasell nuts, at bankets among other dainty fruits' and John Evelyn calls them 'a kinder and better sort of Hazel-nut'. In 1942 the American Committee on Horticulture decided that filbert should be used to describe the cultivated trees, and hazelnut the wild ones, but many still refer to them all as hazels. In Britain hazel can refer to either type, with cob and filbert describing the nut shapes. In practice the trees cross-breed and it is often hard to tell them apart.

The nuts were collected by hunter-gatherers in the Mesolithic era at the end of the Ice Age, with vast numbers of shells being found at the settlements. Easy to grow and easy to harvest, they were one of the first trees used by man. By the Middle Ages they were an important part of the economy, providing much more than just a harvest of nuts. The wood can be bent without breaking, which means it can be woven and was a vital component of wattle and daub houses. Branches were used to make roads, paths and hurdles, and smaller shoots became pea sticks, baskets, fishing rods and traps. The wood burnt well and the smallest twigs were made into faggots for fires or could even be ground and added to ale to encourage fermentation if yeast was not available. The leaves were useful too, mostly as cattle fodder, the belief being that they would encourage the cows to produce more milk.

The nuts are used in sauces in the Roman cookbook of Apicius and are often recommended as an alternative to almonds in early recipe books. They may have been an early theatre snack as vast numbers of shells were found when the Rose Theatre was excavated in London in 1987. They were made into nut liqueurs such as Crème de Noisette and Fratello. Frangelico, an Italian hazelnut liqueur, claims a particularly ancient heritage. The original recipe was apparently created by a hermit, Fra Angelico, and in his honour the bottle is shaped like the habit of a Franciscan friar, with a knotted white cord round the bottle's waist. However, the most famous Fra Angelico, the painter, was a Dominican monk, whose robe would have been white and lacked the cord. Regardless of the inaccurate packaging this is an excellent drink.

By the seventeenth century hazels were grown on a large scale in plats or orchards, particularly in Kent from where they could easily be sent to London by river. In the early nineteenth century Mr Lambert from Goudhurst in Kent introduced a cultivar called 'Lambert's Filbert'. History does not specify which Mr Lambert, so the exact date varies between 1812 and 1830. This became the most popular tree to grow and, confusingly, was known as the Kentish Cob. In Victorian times there were 7,000 acres of hazel orchards or Kentish plats with production reaching its peak just before the First World War. In 1900 there were 4,000 acres of plats in the 'cobnut triangle' between Sevenoaks, Tonbridge and Maidstone but by the late twentieth century this had fallen to a mere 600 acres nationwide. High labour costs had made hazel plats, along with traditional apple and cherry orchards and hop fields, uneconomic. The itinerant pickers who had made their living travelling from harvest to harvest no longer existed and the plants were left to run wild. However more recently with the growing interest in local and traditional foods the Kentish Cobnut Association was founded in 1990. Gradually hazel plats are now being restored to the Kentish countryside.

Hazels have always had magical associations, having the ability to ward off evil and being the wood of choice for wands and divining rods. In China, the nuts were regarded as one of the five sacred nourishments bestowed on humans by the gods and the Roman god Mercury carried a hazel wand. Branches were taken into houses on Midsummer's Eve, the time when the distinction between the natural and supernatural worlds was weakest, for protection against the dark. The wood also gives protection against the lightning of Thor, the god of thunder, and abduction by fairies. The Celts associated the nuts with wisdom and on Nutcrack Night (Hallowe'en) they can be used to foretell the future. Two nuts representing a couple would be placed by the fire; if they jumped it meant that the couple's love would not last, if they remained still while they cooked a long and happy relationship was assured.

They are also apparently responsible for the number of spots on a salmon. Richard Mabey relates this delightful reasoning; near Tipperary there was a beautiful fountain called Connla's Well, overhung by nine hazels. Displaying Beauty and Wisdom, these trees flowered and fruited at the same time, dropping their nuts into the water where the salmon fed on them, the number of spots on the fish corresponding with the number of nuts they had eaten.

According to Peter Treveris' *Grete Herball* of 1526 the nuts would cure a cough if eaten with honey. More unlikely was his claim that crushed husks mixed with 'old grece of a sowe . . . will cause heere to come up in bald places'. Equally questionably a double hazelnut carried in the pocket would apparently cure toothache.

HICKORIES AND PECANS

Part of the walnut family, hickories grow wild in North America. Originally they also grew wild throughout Europe but died out during the last Ice Age. These tall trees grow over 30 m / 100 feet tall and 15 m / 50 feet wide. There are trees thought to be over 1,000 years old which are still producing nuts.

Believed by some Native Americans to represent the Great Spirit, hickories have been a vital source of food for over 8,000 years. The Native American names *paccan*, *pacane* or *pàcan* all mean a nut so hard it must be cracked with a stone and originally applied to all hickories. The nuts were pounded and boiled to produce a kind of nut milk called *powcohicora* and this is where the settlers heard the name they shortened to hickory. Gradually the trees which produced the best nuts came to be called pecans.

Native Americans and settlers alike prized the trees for more than just their nuts. The timber made good building material and the wood was also an excellent fuel for smoking foods. Even the bark was useful, providing a strong yellow dye.

Thomas Jefferson transplanted several hundred trees from Mississippi to his estate at Monticello. He also gave some to George Washington who planted them on 25 March 1777 at Mount Vernon, where they can still be seen.

The first commercial plantation of pecans was planted in Texas in 1880. These plantations are long-term projects; the trees may make you wait up to ten years for the first nuts but will then be profitable for over two hundred. Unfortunately the early growers did not always take this into account and many of the plantations established in the early 1900s went bankrupt while waiting for their first harvest. The nuts are now grown in China, Australia, South Africa, India and Israel but they remain a predominantly American crop, with three-quarters of the world's nuts coming from the States.

The trees have now spread back to Europe, arriving in Britain in 1629. They became popular during the nineteenth century and were granted the attributes of strength and tenacity in the Victorian language of flowers.

MACADAMIAS

These are the native nuts of Australia, originally growing wild in Queensland and northern New South Wales. They were an important source of food to the aborigines, who called them *kindal-kindal*.

Early settlers called them Queensland nuts and tended to be wary of them, justifiably so, as some species are poisonous. Their renown as a food and the name macadamia followed later. In the mid nineteenth century they were 'discovered' by two botanists at the Royal Botanic Gardens, Melbourne, Ferdinand von Mueller and Walter Hill. Keen to grow the trees, they thought that germination rates might improve if the hard shell round the seed was removed. To their horror the assistant tasked with cracking the nuts was found eating them as he worked. He assured his employers how good they were and, still healthy a few days later, proved his point. The nuts were called after the Scottish secretary of the Philosophical Institute of Victoria, Dr John Macadam, and became a commercial crop. The nuts are now also known as Hawaiian nuts as 90% of the worlds' crop are now produced on the island.

OAKS AND ACORNS

The name acorn comes from ac-corn or oak-corn as the nuts could be ground to make a type of flour. In the second century AD the Roman doctor Galen observed that the poor country people used flour made from acorns and this practice continued for centuries. The old English word *aecern* was linked to *aecer* or open country, which eventually led to our land measurement the acre.

The palatability of acorns varies widely. In *Don Quixote* the duchess who befriends the couple writes to Sancho Panza's wife as she has heard that the acorns in her village are particularly fine. Correspondence follows with Teresa, Sancho's wife, regretting that the acorns are small, saying fancifully 'I wish they were as big as ostrich eggs'.

Acorn 'coffee' was drunk during the Second World War when the real thing was scarce. Admittedly we haven't tried it but apparently, while not being true coffee, it is still a perfectly acceptable drink.

According to Culpeper, acorns, leaves and bark could variously be used 'to stop all manner of fluxes' including vomiting, bleeding, poisoning and fevers. John Gerard does not say much about the uses of acorns but oak apples, the growths caused by gall wasps, appear to have a multitude of uses: 'The decoction of Oke Apples steeped in strong white wine vinegar, with a little pouder of Brimstone, and the root of *Ireos* mingled together, and set in the Sun by the space of a moneth, maketh the hair blacke, consumeth proud and superfluous flesh, taketh away sun-burning, freckles, spots, the morphew, with all deformities of the face, being washed therewith.'

Acorn cups, in literature at least, have a whole string of uses. Dodder, the eldest and wisest of B.B.'s *Little Grey Men,* uses one as the base for his false leg and little people throughout history have used them as pipes. They are an invaluable part of any dainty doll's tea service, they make attractive containers for tiny trinkets and are useful drinking vessels, as long as you are small.

From the Roman oak wreaths awarded for valour to the Boscobel Oak in which King Charles II hid in 1651 the trees have a long and venerable history. The magic flute in Mozart's opera was said to be made from a thousand year-old oak and in Rudyard Kipling's poem at the beginning of *Puck of Pook's Hill,* the oak is named as one of the three great trees of Celtic England. Keats and Shakespeare mention the trees and off the coast of Norfolk there is a circle of oak timbers; a Seahenge to rival the better known stone circle. The history of these distinguished trees is beyond the scope of this book but we hope you will research some of the books listed in the Bibliography on page 184.

PEANUTS

The name peanut comes from the fact that they are actually a member of the legume or pea family and ground nut refers to their extraordinary method of growing beneath the ground. The Latin species name, *hypogaea*, also means growing underground. Another common name, the goober pea, comes from the African Bantu name for the nuts, *nguba*. Burl Ives (with Johnny Cash) had an alternative explanation; in a recording of the song *Goober Peas* it is explained that the man who discovered peanuts was a Mr Goober. The popular song was a description of life for the soldiers during the American Civil War; first published in 1866 it humorously credited music to

P. Nutt, Esq. and the words to A. Pindar, Esq. (an American name for peanuts).

Peanuts come from the tropical regions of South America and probably first grew in Peru and Brazil. Pottery vases shaped like peanuts have been found in Inca tombs and the nuts are depicted on the pre-Incan Chimu pottery. They were variously used as food, currency and medicine, with the Aztecs using a peanut paste to relieve

toothache.

The Spanish Conquistadors took the nuts back to Spain and trading ships then took them to Africa where they were traded for spices and elephant tusks. The Portuguese also took them to Africa and fed them to the slaves destined for the Southern USA.

During the American Civil War many northern soldiers developed a taste for peanuts, taking them back north after the fighting was over. By 1900 too many peanuts were being produced so industry came up with a range of new uses. Peanuts are now found in soap, plastics, shaving cream, glue, ink, cosmetics, shoe polish and fertilizer.

Today more peanuts in the USA are used for peanut butter than anything else. The Incas and Aztecs were probably the first peoples to eat it, although they did not give it a name. The first person to patent peanut butter was Marcellus Gilmore Edson, a Canadian, who registered it in 1884. Fourteen years later Dr John Harvey Kellogg, better known for his breakfast cereals, made a similar butter, which started life as a health food, rather than a spread. Nowadays thousands of Americans celebrate National Peanut Butter Day every 24 January.

PISTACHIOS

Pistachios originated in western Asia. Eleven thousand years ago, after the last Ice Age, they reforested the area and then spread west with the campaigns of Alexander the Great. According to Pliny they were brought to Rome by Lucius Vitellius the Elder, the Governor of Syria, in the first century AD. From there they spread to Spain and North Africa. They were probably introduced to Britain in the sixteenth or seventeenth century but did not immediately gain widespread appeal as they could not be successfully cultivated and always remained expensive. They became popular in North America in the 1880s when immigrants brought them to New York city. Now they are mostly grown in the southern states of America and Iran.

Khandan, the Iranian name for the nut, means to laugh, describing the way the nuts seem to smile as they ripen and split open. Their Latin name, *Pistacia vera,* reflects their status and means the true nut, from the Persian. These nuts have always been expensive and highly prized, and there is a rumour accusing the Queen of Sheba of keeping all the nuts in Assyria for herself and her court.

WALNUTS

Walnuts are often regarded as the king of nuts due to their health giving properties. In Greek and Roman mythology the trees belonged to the god Jupiter with their original name *Jovis glans* (being later corrupted to *Juglans*) meaning Jupiter's acorns. In Britain the nuts were originally called Gaul nuts or *wealh* nuts, the Anglo-Saxon for foreign or alien. In France the word *noix,* and in Italy, *noce,* frequently used to refer to nuts in general, actually means only walnuts. In some parts of Germany a peasant farmer had to plant a certain number of walnut trees before he could marry.

The English or Persian walnut originated in Asia and south-east Europe and has been eaten for at least 9,000 years and cultivated for over 2,500. These are not native to Britain but having been here so long, they may predate the Roman occupation, and have adopted the country as their own. There are native walnuts in America but the settlers brought their own to New England and the Persian walnut settled here too, and confusingly became known as the English walnut.

Walnuts were symbols of fertility for the Greek goddess Artemis and the Roman goddess Diana. Romans believed walnuts would ensure good health and fertility and at weddings the bride and groom were showered with the nuts, a practice that survives today. In Medieval Europe the nuts were used as protection against lightning and evil spirits.

The walnut is a classic example of the Doctrine of Signatures, an ancient belief that a plant would cure the part of the body it resembled. Based on this idea the Greeks and Romans believed that walnuts would cure headaches. In the Middle Ages they were used as a cure for epilepsy presumably for the same reason. Strangely enough scientists have since proved that walnuts do 'promote the development of neural transmitters that are vital for brain function'. Nicholas Culpeper, basing the assumption on Pliny the Elder, asserted that Mithridates, King of Pontus, used the following concoction against poisoning and infection: 'Take two dry walnuts, and as many good figs, and twenty leaves of rue, bruised and beaten together with two or three corns of salt, and twenty juniper berries, which, taken every morning fasting, preserves from danger of poison and infection that day it is taken'. According to John Gerard, 'With onions, salt and honey, they are good against the biting of a mad dog or man, if they be laid upon the wound.' Carrying an unshelled walnut in your pocket was said to ease backache, sciatica or rheumatism.

The nuts are mentioned in many early cookery books, as ingredients in fruit pies and sweet and sour meat dishes. Green walnuts were used for pickles, ketchups, liqueurs and syrups. Mrs Beeton includes two recipes for ketchup, one to be made in July when the nuts are still soft, another for September when the hardened nutshells should be soaked for ten days. Vin de Noix is a French aperitif made from the green nuts, Nocino is an Italian liqueur. For some reason it is recommended when making this that you should use an odd number of nuts, ideally thirty-three.

The kernels can be used to remove scratches from walnut furniture; simply rub the nut over the scratch and it will darken and disappear. It is said that an infusion of the husks and leaves, producing a bitter liquid, will remove worms from lawns (although why you would want to do this we don't know; pristine lawns may be an advantage for bowling greens but without worms they won't last long). The oil can be used for cooking or as a painting medium, and the husks and roots produce dye for fabric or hair: yellow from the young green husks or brown from the mature ones.

The wood is often more prized than the nuts. Its beautiful patterns and even strength have made it the choice material for furniture, gun stocks and even, for a time, aeroplane propellers. In 1806 twelve thousand walnut trees were needed every year in France just for the manufacture of muskets. At least two of the suggestions in the rhyme 'Your dog, your wife, your walnut tree, the more you beat them, the better they be' are unacceptable now but the beating of the trees (now fortunately outlawed by the Society for the Protection of Walnut Trees) was believed to create even more intricate patterns in the grain.

Even the shells are highly regarded. In the first century BC in China intricately carved shells which housed crickets, trained to sing on demand, were used as lucky charms. Hans Christian Andersen also used a walnut shell for Thumbelina's cot: 'A finely polished walnut shell formed her cradle, and therein, on a bed of violets, under a rose-leaf coverlet, slept Thumbelina'. When ground, they are a useful abrasive for polishing metal or stone.

NUTCRACKERS

Most nuts need to be cracked open; only pistachios open themselves with an inviting smile. Walnuts can usually be opened by aligning the joints of two nuts together and pressing hard but the seamless hazels

and rock hard Brazils and macadamias need more force. Originally nuts which couldn't be opened by biting were cracked with stones. 'Nutting stones' have been found in Europe and America dating back 8,000 years. These stones had depressions where the nuts were placed and then hit with a 'hammer stone'. Hinged nutcrackers probably date back to Ancient Greece and may have been based on the design of blacksmiths' pincers. The oldest known metal nutcracker dates from the third or fourth century BC and is in the museum in Tarent, Italy. By the fourteenth century they were common in Britain; silver, cast-iron, bronze and wood were the most usual materials, although one or two porcelain examples survive.

In the seventeenth century the development of screw nutcrackers allowed a more gentle pressure to be applied and reduced the risk of shattering the kernels. As a course of fruits and nuts at dinner became more widespread, so nutcrackers became more ornate. Designs of figures and animals were prevalent, particularly around the Alps where they were sold as souvenirs. Soldiers, knights and kings who bit down on the nuts with their over-sized mouths and sharp teeth were the most popular and in Germany they were a good luck symbol which would protect your home.

E. T. A. Hoffmann's tale *The Nutcracker* was first published in 1816. The story became the basis for Tchaikovsky's ballet and after its premiere in St Petersburg in 1892 the story, albeit slightly altered, was assured immortality. In both versions the Nutcracker, the hero of the tale, comes alive to do battle against the evil Mouse King. After this the stories diverge but always, as a dashing soldier, the boy is handsome. In his previous life as a wooden nutcracker his looks are less impressive:

> It must be confessed, a great deal could not be said in favour of the beauty of his figure, for not only was his rather broad, stout body, out of all proportion to the little, slim legs that carried it, but his head was by far too large for either. A genteel dress went a great way to compensate for these defects, and led to the belief that he must be a man of taste and good breeding. He wore a hussar's jacket of beautiful bright violet, fastened together with white loops and buttons, pantaloons of exactly the same colour, and the neatest boots that ever graced the foot of a student or officer. They fitted as tight to his little legs as if they were painted upon them. . . . Nothing but kindness and benevolence shone in his clear green, though somewhat too prominent eyes.
>
> It was very becoming to the man that he wore about his chin a nicely trimmed beard of white cotton, for by this the sweet smile upon his deep red lips was rendered much more striking. . . . Father . . . . raised up his wooden cloak, whereupon the little man stretched his mouth wide open, and showed two rows of very sharp white teeth.

Industrial production meant that nutcrackers became cheaper and more widespread. In 1913 the spring-jointed nutcracker was patented by the delightfully named Henry Quackenbush of Herkimer, New York and in 1947 the Crackerjack was patented by Cuthbert Leslie Rimes of Morley, Leeds, and exhibited at the Festival of Britain. This worked on the same principle as a car jack, with the pressure being increased very slowly thus minimizing the risk of damaging the kernel.

In the 1960s the increased availability of pre-shelled nuts led to the decline of the need for nutcrackers and many languished at the back of drawers. Nuts were also less common in children's Christmas stockings. Originally they would have been a great luxury but by the late twentieth century they had largely been replaced with chocolates and other sweets.

Nutcrackers are now more likely to be found in collectors' display cabinets than on dining tables or in museums such as that at Leavenworth, a recreated Bavarian village in Washington.

AND LASTLY

'As nutty as a fruitcake', 'you're off your nut', 'you belong in a nuthouse', 'I'm nuts about him', 'a hard nut to crack'. In a nutshell, nuts can indicate lunacy, passion, scorn or disappointment; they can refer to testicles or someone's head. Meanwhile, nutters have changed their behaviour and the charming verb nutting has largely died out. Perhaps now is the time to reinstate it.

> The sun had stooped his westward clouds to win
> Like weary traveller seeking for an Inn
> When from the hazelly wood we glad descried
> The ivied gateway by the pasture side
> Long had we sought for nuts amid the shade
> Where silence fled the rustle that we made
> When torn by briars and brushed by sedges rank
> We left the wood and on the velvet bank
> Of short sward pasture ground we sat us down
> To shell our nuts before we reached the town

(From *Nutting* by John Clare)

NUTS FOR HEALTH

Let thy food be thy medicine and thy medicine be thy food.

(Hippocrates)

Humans have been eating nuts ever since we started eating. The earliest hunter gatherers quickly recognized the benefits of easy sustenance and the flavour offered by nuts. What they may have not realized is that those same nuts were a great healthy eating choice. You tended to be less picky about your diet way back when half your life was spent dodging predators and the rest devoted to finding enough to keep yourself alive. If it was tasty, not poisonous and didn't bite back, adding it to the diet was a no-brainer.

Recent studies of nuts however have firmly established their position as a healthy eating choice. A *New England Journal of Medicine* study of 120,000 people over 30 years found that eating nuts helped to increase lifespan. People who ate nuts at least once a week were 11% less likely to have died prematurely than those who never ate nuts; indeed when nut consumption increased to a daily portion, the benefit increased to 50%. Similar positive effects from nut consumption were reported by the Iowa Women's Study and the Harvard Nurses' Study. The main reduction was in death from heart disease but there was also an appreciable drop in deaths from cancer. As always with these studies it is impossible to isolate findings entirely as those following a high nut diet often tended to be predisposed to other healthy lifestyle choices as well.

We would also like to stress that when looking at food and diet you should always be aware there is no magic bullet. You cannot eat whatever you like in huge quantities and just add one tiny spoonful of this or a single wonder bean to counteract a series of poor choices. Chow down on a family-sized bucket of fried chicken washed down by six beers every night and one little peanut isn't going to save you however hard he tries. Where nuts excel are as delicious, satisfying treats which deliver the flavour and texture of processed snack foods but without the accompanying E-numbers. Because they are nutrient dense you will feel fuller and, let's be honest, a bowl of kale was never going to work as an indulgent sofa snack. Build nuts into your diet and you will be healthier; just don't try to use them as a roadblock on that culinary road to perdition.

Nuts and Fat

Nuts are extremely nutritious, in fact behind pure fats and oils they are the highest calorie food we can eat, delivering huge amounts of energy in a small parcel. This is one reason they are perfect emergency stores, light to carry, difficult to damage or spoil and delivering an immediate shot of energy. It is no wonder that most hikers carry a small bag of nuts with them on treks.

The flip side of this is that they are high in calories, and 80% of a nut is fat. That said the fats they contain are the poly- and mono-unsaturated heart-friendly type and the skins on nuts are tremendously high in fibre.

There is a slightly Orwellian situation where some nuts are more equal than others in the fat stakes. Creamy nuts such as Brazils, macadamias and cashews are high in saturated fats; walnuts, peanuts and pistachios sit in the middle, and hazelnuts, almonds and cashews are at the lower end of the scale. Do remember though that we are talking raw nuts here, if they are highly flavoured and salted or covered in chocolate then this will make a difference. The nuts themselves will still be healthy but unless you are giving them a good rinse first, the baggage they bring with them may affect their nutritional value (no point trying to fool yourself, we have been there, a chocolate covered nut is confectionery not health food). Current guidelines which strongly recommend incorporating nuts in a healthy diet recommend four to five servings a week (a serving is a small handful, 1.5 oz, of raw nuts or 2 tablespoons of nut butter).

If you are counting calories then the only low-fat nut is the chestnut. It is also worth noting if you are concerned about the potential calorific fallout from increasing nuts in your diet, that many nuts are rich sources of arginine. Arginine inhibits fat absorption and the higher the arginine content, the lower the cholesterol.

It is also believed that the high fibre content in nuts means that they pass through the body without being completely broken down, possibly a case of having your walnut cake and eating it.

Nuts and Fibre

Fibre works to lower cholesterol, is thought to play a role in the prevention of diabetes and is essential to digestive health. Because nuts are high in fibre and protein, they make us feel fuller. This is why a handful (a small handful) of nuts is a good snack. The National Health Service (NHS) advises including 18 grams of fibre in your daily diet but many people seem to struggle to achieve this. Nuts, particularly almonds, pecans and walnuts, are high in fibre and a handful a day is a quick and tasty way of increasing your fibre intake.

Vitamins, Minerals and Trace Elements

Nuts provide many of the disease-fighting vitamins and minerals we need in our daily lives. All nuts are rich sources of iron, zinc and magnesium. Some nuts, notably Brazils are exceptionally high in selenium, an antioxidant mineral which helps protect against heart disease, slow down the effects of ageing and has been cited as beneficial in preventing some cancers.

Nuts provide a wide range of essential vitamins and minerals including several B group vitamins, vitamin E and minerals such as calcium iron, zinc potassium, magnesium, selenium manganese and copper. Vitamin E, present in hazelnuts and almonds in particular, is a valuable antioxidant, the key to a strong immune system and a positive contributor to skin and eye health. Modern diets are frequently deficient in vitamin E and nuts and nut butters can be a tasty way to boost your intake. Nuts are low in sodium (provided you avoid salted nuts of course).

Nuts and Heart Health

Although nuts are comparatively high in calories, their fat content is unsaturated fat, thought to lower cholesterol levels. Nuts are one of the best plant-based sources of omega 3 fatty acids. Studies have suggested that consuming 30 grams of nuts a day can reduce your risk of heart disease by up to 50%. There are a number of heart-healthy attributes in nuts which contribute to this, chiefly the monounsaturated and polyunsaturated fats which mitigate against blood cholesterol but also the fibre content, antioxidant vitamins and minerals (including vitamin E, copper, manganese, selenium and zinc) that reduce oxidation and inflammation, and the naturally low sodium and high potassium levels which maintain healthy blood pressure.

A lesser known benefit from increased nut consumption is the role that they play in improving the health and efficiency of your arteries. All nuts are high in vitamin E and vitamin E helps prevent the build-up of plaque on arterial walls. Nuts are also high in plant sterols. These are added to margarines and products marketed as heart-healthy and cholesterol-reducing but it is so much better to get those benefits where they occur naturally. Finally nuts are a great source of L-arginine which boosts the health, strength and flexibility of your arterial walls and reduces the build-up of clots within arteries which left unchecked may lead to heart attacks.

Nut Allergies

Unfortunately a small number of people, around 1-2% of the population, are allergic to nuts. This is a serious allergy and can be life threatening. People with nut allergies are almost invariably aware of their condition. Never include nuts in a dish without letting people know. This is particularly the case if you are using a nut substitute for another ingredient (for example using nut milk in place of cow's milk, or ground nuts in place of flour.)

There are differing views on the early exposure of children to nut products. It used to be believed that nuts should be excluded from the diet of very young children; however more recently there is a school of thought which suggests that the gradual introduction of a wide variety of foods, including nuts, from a young age is the more beneficial path and avoids the development of allergies later. It is generally safest (and contributes to a quiet life) to follow the guidance of the parents. Whole nuts are usually not given to children under five, not so much from fear of health problems as from the danger of them choking or putting them up their noses (luckily we grow out of this tendency fairly quickly).

Nuts and Special Diets

Nuts are a lifesaver for those on special diets. Nut milks are ideal for those with a dairy allergy and ground nuts can be used instead of flour in cakes and baking for those who are condemned to a gluten-free diet.

Flavonoids and Antioxidants

Flavonoids are not some futuristic race of kitchen robots but phytonutrients found in most fruits and vegetables. There are over 6,000 different types. Flavonoids are the secret powerhouses behind the success of the Mediterranean diet. They are powerful antioxidants with immense anti-inflammatory and immune system benefits. Antioxidants counter the free radicals and toxins which form naturally in the body as we age. Eating diets with high quantities of flavonoid-containing foods has been recommended to reduce the incidence of cancer, neurodegenerative and cardiovascular disease. Interestingly the effect of flavonoids is strongest when the products containing them are eaten raw, as in some cases up to 80% of the flavonoids in foods can be lost in cooking.

Walnuts and pecans are high in the flavonoid anthocyanidin while pistachios and cashews are high in catechin. Anthocyandin, also present in many dark berries, works to counter cardiovascular disease and cancer and to boost cognitive function. It is believed to inhibit neuroinflammation and improve blood flow to the brain improving memory and slowing age related cognitive degeneration. Catechin is the plant-based antioxidant which is considered to deliver the health benefits of green tea. It is particularly effective in fighting free radicals which cause disease and the ageing effects caused by cellular degeneration.

Almonds

Almonds have excellent calcium levels. This is one reason almond milk is such a great substitute for those following a dairy-free diet as it can help provide the bone-strengthening benefits of calcium which can be lacking in dairy-free diets. It has a rich unctuous mouth feel too which we have found lacking in many other dairy-free 'milks'. Almonds are one of the nuts we most commonly eat with the skin on, boosting the benefits received from their significant fibre content.

Brazil Nuts

Brazil nuts are the richest food source of selenium. As few as three

Brazil nuts a day can provide your RDA (Recommended Daily Allowance). Selenium is a trace mineral which helps build a healthy immune system and boost fertility. Recent studies have suggested that selenium may also protect against bone, prostate and breast cancers.

Cashews

Cashews are rich in copper which is good for bones and nerves. One serving of cashews provides a person's entire RDA of copper. Copper works in the body to manufacture red blood cells and form collagen, a key component in building bones and connective tissue. A Harvard University study also suggested that eating cashews may guard against the development of gallstones, possibly because of the link between gallstones and high cholesterol.

Sweet Chestnuts

Chestnuts are the lowest in fat and calories but pack a punch in terms of carbohydrates and fibre. Unlike most nuts which have a high oil content, chestnuts have an unusually (for a nut) high proportion of water. They are also (surprisingly - have you ever seen an orange chestnut?) a good source of vitamin C.

Chestnuts also have a high starch content. In cooking this means you can use them as you would carbohydrate foods like potatoes, sweet potatoes or plantains. In common with many other nuts they contain no gluten; this coupled with starch means they grind to an excellent flour which can be used effectively in cakes, pastries and breads by those with wheat allergies or coeliac disease.

Historically chestnuts, and more often the bark of the chestnut tree, have been used as an effective remedy for diarrhoea. Three tablespoons of chestnuts (whole including the shell) crushed up and boiled for 20 minutes in a litre of water is the standard treatment. This may be a result of the tannin in the shells.

Hazelnuts

Hazelnuts are rich in folate which helps regulate our homocysteine levels guarding against heart disease and conditions like Parkinson's disease. Folate counters anaemia and neural tube defects in the newborn. A diet rich in folates is recommended for women seeking to conceive and for expectant mothers.

Hazelnut oil is considered especially enriching for the skin and is often included in skin creams and cosmetics.

Pecans

Pecans have high levels of those plant sterols effective at lowering cholesterol levels. In common with avocados and olives, they are high in oleic acid.

They have good levels of B3 which is useful in accessing energy and fighting fatigue. If you are driving distances, a bag of nuts in the glove compartment is your friend. They will give you that energy boost without the sugar spike and can counteract fatigue.

Pistachios

Pistachios are particularly rich in B6, excellent for hormone balance and mood regulation. They are also the only nut to contain reasonable levels of lutein and zeaxanthin for eye health.

Excitingly pistachios are considered one of the less fattening nuts at less than 4 calories each (and if you buy them shell-on and factor in the energy taken to get them out of the shell we feel they could be right up there with celery).

They are an excellent source of potassium which is good for the immune system.

A recent Spanish study reported that patients who regularly ate pistachios found it easier to regulate their blood sugar.

Walnuts

Walnuts are high in antioxidants and monounsaturated fats. They also contain high levels of manganese which may reduce PMS symptoms. The anti-inflammatory and pain relieving properties of omega 3 may also play a role here and explain why a good handful of walnuts has been cited as an old wives' remedy to alleviate the pain of menstrual cramps.

They are the only nut to offer a significant dose of alpha-linolenic acid, an omega 3 fatty acid that delivers heart and brain health benefits. Due to the high antioxidant content walnuts may reduce the risk of Alzheimer's disease.

Walnuts have been used in Chinese medicine for centuries. Because they are believed to look like the brain (we can see that) they are considered good for mental health. They are also believed to invigorate qi (the life source or vital energy), enrich the blood, nourish muscle and amazingly to blacken hair (clearly the Chinese answer to eating your crusts to get curly hair).

NUTS IN THE WILD

Foraging is the oldest occupation of humankind.
For most of our history we knew no other way of living.

(Samuel Thayer, *The Forager's Harvest*)

One of the joys of foraging for nuts is that you can call yourself a nutter. Strictly speaking, this refers to the harvesters of cobnuts but can be used to describe anyone harvesting any type of nuts. This section is intended to encourage you to go out and look for nuts but it is not a definitive guide. We have only included nuts you are likely to find on an average walk. Brazil nuts are the ultimate wild nut, defying attempts to cultivate them but you are not very likely to find them on a Sunday afternoon stroll.

In these days of easy availability you will probably not be foraging for survival. This does not in any way detract from the pleasure of finding a free harvest and, in some cases, the harvests you find will avoid the need to visit the shops. Whatever your reason for foraging there are one or two things to bear in mind.

Firstly, you must be absolutely certain what you are collecting or eating. Anything that only looks 'roughly like the picture' should be left. Some trees are easy to recognise but for most foraging expeditions a good guide is vital; either in the form of a reliable book or a person. Ideally use at least two guide books so you can compare the descriptions.

The laws relating to foraging are, to say the least, complex. In Scotland there are statutory access rights and you can walk almost anywhere. In North America the laws of trespass are strict and often rigorously enforced. England and much of Europe wavers in between. And this is before you have even thought of picking anything. On the whole common sense is the best guide. If the land is clearly owned by someone, seek permission before harvesting. Don't cause damage and don't strip the trees bare; remember some birds and animals may depend on the crop for survival. Pick thoughtfully; there is a huge difference between collecting a few nuts to roast and harvesting a sufficient quantity to make enough oil to last you through the winter.

Pollution isn't usually a problem for nuts as they are encased in shells. Even so, avoid agricultural areas that may have been recently sprayed and busy roads. Again most of this is common sense; picking nuts from the quiet side of the hedge will be preferable and safer than balancing on the edge of a main road.

In most countries it is illegal to dig up plants that are growing in the wild, as well as those in parks and gardens. This applies to all those enticing-looking seedlings round the base of the tree. Either grow your own from seed or buy a plant from a nursery. There is considerable debate as to whether foraging helps or harms the countryside. As long as you forage sensibly we are firmly of the opinion that it helps. As Richard Mabey said, 'No one is going to stand by whilst the hedge which provides his sloe gin is bulldozed down.' Foraging makes people more aware of the plants and their environment and, on the whole, once we notice something we are more likely to want to protect it. The introduction of invasive species, urban and industrial sprawl and the indiscriminate spraying of chemicals are all far greater risks to the fragile balance of nature.

What you use to collect your harvest is up to you. Trugs and baskets look charming, plastic bags are useful, if unattractive. In recent years folding cotton bags have become widespread and, for most nuts these are a good option. The best nuts are nearly always just out of reach. A stout walking stick is an innocent looking accessory but it will give you an extra 3-4 feet of reach, either to gently knock or pull down crop-laden branches. A hat is invaluable; it will keep you cool or dry depending on the season and will give protection from falling nuts when you shake the trees to encourage the ripe ones to fall. Finally, an unusual piece of equipment suggested by John Wright is a car. Park it beneath your chosen tree, climb onto the roof and suddenly it is as if you are on stilts.

THE FORAGING YEAR

This is a rough guide to harvesting times:

Mid summer: wet walnuts
Early autumn: hazels, wet walnuts
Mid autumn: beech mast, sweet chestnuts, hazels, hickories, acorns, walnuts
Late autumn: beech mast, sweet chestnuts, acorns, walnuts.

THE NUTS

Below is a selection of some of the best nuts to forage. Some of these trees you will find growing wild in the countryside, others can be found in parks and gardens. Many of the cultivated trees may be grown for their structure, flowers or leaf colour and can be excellent places to find a hidden harvest.

BEECHES AND BEECH MAST (*Fagus* spp.)

The fruits of the beech tree are often called beech mast, or just mast, and the latter name is also sometimes confusingly used to refer to acorns. Traditionally used as animal fodder, beech mast is something you are unlikely to find in shops but it is well worth harvesting.

The trees are tall, growing up to 30 m / 100 feet, they grow in temperate regions and have spread into the wild. The common beech (*Fagus sylvatica*) and the American beech (*F. grandiflora*) are the species you are most likely to find, either in parks and gardens or woodland.

The triangular nuts grow in a bright green oval husk which is shaggy at first, becoming more bristly as the fruit ripens, eventually resembling a small parcel made of door matting. When the nuts are ripe the case splits open revealing up to four rich brown nuts. Closed husks are worth collecting as they will often open a few days later if stored somewhere dry. There is a fairly short foraging season as the early husks to fall are usually unripe and the ripe nuts are popular with squirrels, mice, badgers and deer. Mid to late autumn is the time to look. One way is to spread a sheet beneath the tree and give it a good shake but, given the size of some trees, this isn't always an option. Don't be disappointed if a tree which produced a spectacular harvest one year is barren the next; beech trees usually only crop well every three to four years, sometimes even less.

The nuts are small and fiddly to peel so harvesting is a time-consuming but not unpleasant affair. Depending on the shell, you can peel it or bash it on an edge with a hammer and remove the nut meat with a nut pick. They are mildly toxic if eaten straight from the tree. One of the best ways to eat beech mast is to fry the nuts in butter or oil and sprinkle with salt. Another option is to use them to flavour gin, in the same way as you would use sloes or damsons. In southern Europe the mast is used to make oil, which is lovely and sweet and keeps well but you need a lot of nuts for this. Ideally you should peel each shell and scrape away the skin as this can make the oil bitter. Then pulverize the nuts in an electric grinder and squeeze through muslin. You can also use the mast to make a hot drink, sometimes called 'coffee'. It is nothing like coffee but quite pleasant, in an acquired way.

Sweet Chestnut (*Castanea* spp.)

Sweet or Spanish chestnuts (*C. sativa*) grow into large deciduous trees, reaching up to 30 m / 100 feet if not coppiced. It is these large trees that are the best to forage from as coppiced trees bear less fruit. Sweet chestnuts are widespread through most temperate regions and before chestnut blight struck in the 1900s, one in four trees in eastern North America was an American chestnut (*C. dentata*). Many of these trees have now grown new shoots from the old stumps but are not particularly productive. European and Asian trees are resistant to the blight, and it is these where you will probably find the best harvests.

The chestnuts you find for sale in shops will probably have been commercially produced in southern Europe or California. The nuts you find in the wild will be smaller but no less tasty. In John Evelyn's time, chestnuts were frequently fed to swine but as he pointed out they were 'amongst the delicacies of princes in other countries'.

The husks of a sweet chestnut are pale green and covered in fine spines, earning them the common name 'hedgehogs'. They start to drop from the trees in early autumn but many of these first husks will be empty or contain flattened or whitish nuts which are not worth harvesting. This is the tree's way of enabling it to concentrate its energies on producing a better harvest of larger nuts. The main crop comes in mid autumn, by which time the husk will contain 2-3 roundish, triangular nuts. When they are ripe they are a slightly dull brown colour and are covered with very fine hairs. Thomas Hardy describes them in *The Woodlanders*: 'The burst husks of chestnuts lay exposing their auburn contents as if arranged by anxious sellers in a fruit-market.'

Collecting chestnuts is one of the times when it is worth wearing stout gardening gloves (not woollen ones which offer no protection) as the spines on the husks will work their way painfully in to any exposed skin. The trees are usually too tall and solid to shake but a walking stick can be used to dislodge husks that are almost ready to fall. Wear a hat unless you want spiny bombs falling painfully on your head. The easiest way to break open the husks is to put them in a pile on the ground and roll them with a stoutly-booted foot. The ripe husks will then easily split open revealing the nuts.

Once you peel away the shell and pith, the kernels can be eaten raw and, depending on the tree, may be deliciously sweet and tender or tough and dull. Most chestnuts are much better roasted. According to Pliny, 'Chestnuts are better roasted than cooked in any other manner'. Make a small cut in each nut shell to stop it exploding and then put them in the embers of a fire or in an oven at 200°C / 400 F / Gas 6. Some books recommend leaving one nut to explode as an indicator of when they are ready but we've found that this is a rather lethal and unnecessary guide as the cuts split open when the nuts are ready. John Gerard has this charming warning in his *Herball* of 1597, 'they have in them a certain windinesse, and by reason of this, unless the shell be first cut, they skip suddenly with a cracke out of the fire whilst they be rosting'.

If you don't want to leave anything to chance, you can invest in a chestnut roaster. This is basically a long-handled skillet with a lid. The lid has small holes which allow the steam to escape but prevents the exploding nuts from showering everyone with hot shards of nutshell. The nuts are easiest to peel when still hot, although obviously cool enough to handle.

The nuts can also be used in soups, stuffing, as marrons glacés or ground as flour. In mountainous regions round the Mediterranean, chestnut flour is often used, as the trees can survive at higher altitudes than wheat. It is fragrant but does not rise well so if you need a rise use half chestnut and half wheat flour.

To store chestnuts for Christmas you need to put the nuts in a bag which will breathe but not rot and bury them in the soil. Hessian or sacking works well and will keep the nuts fresh and moist. They will be perfect for Christmas but if left in the ground in spring they will start to sprout as the soil warms up.

Horse chestnuts (*Aesculus hippocastanum*), despite the similar sounding common name, are completely different trees and produce nuts which are not edible. Like many nuts these were roasted and ground in an attempt to imitate coffee during the Second World War but apparently produced a truly disgusting drink. They are easy to distinguish as horse chestnut husks have short, hard spines and contain a single, shiny, brown nut. Ideal for playing conkers but not to be eaten.

Hazels and Hazelnuts (*Corylus* spp.)

The problem with hazelnuts is that in mid autumn they are everyone's favourite food; you will need to get to the trees before squirrels, mice and a host of birds. To make matters worse squirrels will take the nuts when they are still green; this is very annoying for human foragers but also detrimental for the tree population as the green nuts are not sufficiently ripe to set seed. As a remedy for this John Wright suggests eating squirrels, recommending squirrel offal kebabs but, of course, first you have to catch your squirrel.

Hazels are small, deciduous trees, rarely growing more than 6 m / 20 feet tall. You will find them in hedges or planted in clusters for coppicing but the best trees for nuts are those in woodlands, parks or gardens, which have been allowed to grow to their full size. They are native to Europe and do well in all temperate regions including much of North America. The trees are easy to recognise in winter with their bright yellow catkins and it is worth noting the trees then so you can return later in the year for the harvest.

Most trees growing in Britain and Europe are cobnuts (*C. avellana*) or filberts (*C. maxima*). The two are closely related and will interbreed if planted close together. *C. maxima* 'Purpurea' is a commonly cultivated tree as its leaves and catkins are prettily tinged with a magenta-purple. The papery bracts are the same attractive colour and are sometimes overlooked by squirrels. In North America you will also find the beaked hazelnut (*C. cornuta*) and the American hazelnut (*C. americana*).

The nuts come in clusters of 2-4 and are surrounded by a husk of papery bracts which looks like an upturned frilly bonnet. In filberts the nuts are slightly longer and are completely encased in the husk. As they ripen both the nuts and bracts turn brown. They can be easy to miss as the clusters often grow beneath the leaves which turn yellow at the same time as the nuts ripen. They are ready to pick in early autumn; St. Philibert's Day, after whom filberts are called, falls on 20 August but this is usually too early for a decent crop. The nuts can be picked from the tree or, if it is in the open, a good shake will reveal all the ripe nuts. It is worth checking the husks as you open them; some will be 'blank' or 'hedge' nuts, a term used by Kentish growers to describe an empty husk. Pretty as they are you do not want to arrive home proudly carrying a basket of empty ones.

The early green nuts can be eaten and are soft and milky-tasting. Once picked they will not continue to ripen and do not store well so you will need to eat them immediately. Mature nuts will keep for several months; leave them in their shells and store in a warm, dry, mouse- and squirrel-free place. They can be used in salads, ground for use in baking or, our favourite, coated in caramel and used to decorate cakes and puddings.

Hickories and Pecans (*Carya* spp.)

Hickories grow wild throughout North America but are more likely to be found in parks and gardens in Britain and Europe. They reach up to 30 m / 100 feet and their ornamental bark and autumn colours are often more highly prized than their fruits.

Pecans (*C. illinoinensis*) are the kings of hickories but they are not reliably hardy and need long, warm summers to ripen the nuts. Shagbark hickories (*C. ovata*) have thick, oval-shaped husks which encase 6 cm / 2.5 inch long nuts which are excellent to eat. Those of the bitternut or swamp hickory (*C. cordiformis*) are round and unpalatable and nuts from hognuts or pignuts (*C. glabra*) are longer but equally unpalatable. The nuts fall to the ground in early autumn and the husks usually split open naturally, making harvesting reasonably easy.

The nuts can be eaten raw or used in any sweet baking. The wood from hickory trees is commonly used in smoking food where it imparts a delicious flavour.

Oaks and Acorns (*Quercus* spp.)

Oaks are one of the most easily recognised trees with their distinctive wavy-edged leaves and majestic shape. They can be found in mixed woodland, pollarded within hedges or as specimen trees in parks and gardens. They originally come from Europe, western Asia and North Africa and can now be found growing cultivated and wild in all temperate regions. In Britain and Europe there are three main types of oak which can easily be distinguished by their acorns. The common or English oak (*Q. robur*) has acorn cups which grow on stalks, sessile oaks (*Q. petraea*) have acorn cups without stalks, and Turkey oaks (*Q. cerris*) have bristly cups and jagged leaves. The only confusion which may occur is when common and sessile oaks are planted close together and hybridize.

In North America oaks divide into white oaks (most commonly the white oak, *Q. alba*) and red oaks (rather confusingly the most common is the black oak, *Q. velutina*) which have rounder acorns. Both can be harvested in early autumn; those on the white oaks tend to be sweeter.

As they ripen the acorn and cups change from green to brown, dropping to the ground in autumn, usually just before the leaves fall. For thousands of years many people regarded acorns as vital food, both for themselves and their animals. Pannage was a traditional right that was granted to the residents of a forest allowing their pigs to forage for acorns. This was doubly useful as it removed the danger for cattle and horses for whom the tannins in acorns are poisonous. These tannins mean that acorns are also inedible for humans until they have been leached out. Repeatedly boiling the kernels in fresh water until it runs clean is one way, or you can use the Native American method of burying the nuts in the ground. This is a longer term method as the nuts need to be left in the ground over winter.

Despite their long history as an important food, acorns are rarely eaten now. They can be ground and roasted to make a drink often referred to as 'coffee'. As John Lewis-Stempel points out in his book *Foraging*, this produces a perfectly palatable drink, even though it tastes nothing like coffee. The cups are, of course, still collected by children for dainty dolls' tea sets and by gnomes to use as pipes.

Walnuts (*Juglans* spp.)

Walnuts grow up to 30 m / 100 feet tall and are native to China, western and central Asia and southern Europe. They have now naturalized in most temperate regions and although most of the trees you find will have been planted, some will have grown from seed. The most widespread species are the common, English or Persian walnut (*J. regia*) and, in North America, the black walnut (*J. nigra*) and butternut (*J. cinerea*), but fruit from any walnut tree can be eaten.

Walnuts can be picked 'wet' or 'dry'. Wet walnuts are young fruits and are usually ready to harvest in mid summer. It is worth wearing rubber gloves to harvest these nuts as the oil contains a brown dye which will stain your fingers. At this stage the nuts and their cases are soft, green and aromatic; you should be able to pierce them with a sharp knife. These do not keep well and are best pickled (see our recipe on page 108).

The main harvest will ripen in mid to late autumn and the cases will gradually harden and turn brown. At this point most ripe nuts will fall, although a little shake or a prod with a stick can also be used to encourage any that might be on the point of falling. Spread the nuts out and leave for a few days during which time the outer husk will soften and can be peeled away, again wearing rubber gloves unless you want brown hands. This will reveal the hard nutshell, which can usually be cracked by taking two nuts, aligning the seams and pressing hard. Failing that you can use nut crackers or a well-aimed bash with a hammer. It is often easiest to extract the nut itself using a nut pick.

Walnuts are delicious eaten raw, particularly with blue cheese. They are probably the most commonly used nut in cooking with a wide variety of sweet and savoury applications. They will also keep well once shelled; for several months in a refrigerator and up to a year in a deep freeze.

NUTS IN THE GARDEN

Large streams from little fountains flow,
Tall oaks from little acorns grow.

(David Everett, *Lines Written for a School Declamation*)

One of the best things you can do in a garden is plant a tree. Assuming you are in a position to do so, how much better to plant a tree that offers you the promise of a delicious harvest. Many gardens contain an apple or pear tree, far too few contain a nut tree.

Many nut trees are large and long-lived and are a plant for the future as much as the present. You may be planting a tree which will grow a hundred feet tall and live for hundreds, perhaps even thousands, of years. It requires a bit of a leap of faith to do this rather than plant some annuals but leaps of faith are what gardening is all about; if you have the space (and you may not need as much as you think), please plant a nut tree; your grandchildren will thank you.

Not all the nuts covered in the recipe section of this book are practical for the average garden, delicious though they may be, and so we have concentrated here on the trees that will thrive in temperate regions rather than those that require tropical heat. We have also given most space to the smaller almonds and hazels, which are within the reach of most gardens.

Hazels grow into compact trees and, if you can beat the squirrels, will provide you with a delicious harvest of nuts. Almonds are also small, extremely pretty trees, with delightful spring blossom and the promise of nuts in good years. Sweet chestnuts and walnuts grow into grand majestic trees and although they are not suited to every garden they are among the best trees to choose if you have the space. Oaks and beeches also need space and may not instantly spring to mind when you are considering an edible harvest but they are both wonderful trees, with the added bonus of acorns and mast. Hickories, including pecans, and pistachios will only suit certain climates and can be unpredictable, but hickories are beautiful trees and anyone who would consider growing an olive should certainly give a home to an equally charming pistachio tree. Finally there are peanuts, very much the odd ones out in this group. Botanically they are not even nuts but belong to the pea family. They grow as annuals, their flowers dipping down to ground level to allow the nuts to develop beneath the soil, curiosities indeed but a fun project well worth considering for almost any garden.

NUT TREES IN YOUR GARDEN

You can plant nut trees as individual specimens, create nut walks, grow plats or cultivate coppices. To a certain extent it will depend on the amount of space you have and the tree you choose; an orchard of full-sized sweet chestnuts would be huge. Walnuts and sweet chestnuts in particular make beautiful specimen trees in the middle of a lawn, or parkland if you are lucky enough to own such a thing.

Plats are traditional Kentish orchards of hazels. The trees were often kept as low as 2 m / 6 feet tall but trained to spread as wide as 6 m / 20 feet. These peculiar looking trees were very easy to harvest from and cropped well.

Nuttery is a looser term and can be used to describe almost any planting of nuts. In many large gardens these, or nut walks, led into the main fruit orchard. The nut walk at Munstead Wood was planted by Gertrude Jekyll in 1887 and the famous one at Sissinghurst in Kent was based on the same idea.

Hazels and sweet chestnuts can also be coppiced. Traditionally this was used to provide the poles and supports for medieval wattle and daub houses. The thinner stems were woven between the poles to create a lattice against which daub (a mixture of soil, animal dung and straw) was smeared to create a solid wall. Even the twigs were used, as fuel in bakers' ovens. For many years coppicing was an important part of the rural economy, providing everything from clothes pegs to hurdles and pea sticks. After the First World War rising labour costs and cheap imports heralded the economic end of widespread coppicing. The regular cutting creates a natural cycle whereby light and warmth regularly reach the ground, rejuvenating the whole area. It is a very good way to grow hazels as the cutting process provides constant change and interest in the garden. You don't even need much space, a coppice can consist of just two or three trees.

Coppiced trees, and indeed all hazels, are ideal for growing in a meadow with wild flowers and bulbs or with low understory planting. As the trees lose their leaves in winter there is enough light for early flowers to thrive. Snowdrops, chionodoxa and scilla look magical under the bare branches in the low winter light. Bluebells, primroses and wood anemones complement the new lime green leaves in spring and aquilegias and tiarellas will complete the picture in summer. When the trees grow up and cast more shade, ferns and lily of the valley provide a perfect understory.

GROWING NUTS

Unlike many vegetables and herbs, most nut trees will live for many years, probably outliving you and your children. It is therefore worth spending a little time considering the practicalities and choosing the right varieties to put in the right places. Specific requirements are given within the sections on individual nuts.

SITE

Most nuts do best in a sunny, sheltered site, many are wind-pollinated but this means a gentle breeze, not a gale that will blow all the pollen away. Most also have long taproots and need deep, well-drained soil, although hazels are more shallow-rooted and actually fruit better on poor stony soil.

Much of northern Europe and North America have perfect climates for growing nut trees. The only problem may be late spring frosts as many trees, and almonds in particular, blossom early in the year. It is often best to plant trees on a slight slope rather than in a hollow which could be a frost pocket, trapping cold air in the winter. For small trees, a south-facing wall can provide the necessary protection, as can horticultural fleece, which can be draped over the plant if frost is forecast at a crucial time. The blossom is obviously vulnerable, as too are the little nuts when they first form.

CHOOSING THE NUTS

When referring to nut trees, most people simply use the common names (hazel, almond, walnut etc.) but each one has its own Latin name, written in two parts (*Juglans regia* or common walnut). This system is used worldwide and ensures that you know exactly which plant is which. It may seem like a bit of a palaver but similar sounding trees can vary enormously in size and character. The first part of the name is the genus and, horticulturally, this is the most important division. All plants are categorized into larger families but these are of more interest to the botanist than the gardener. The second word is the species and is a further subdivision within the genus. Peaches, plums and almonds all belong within the *Prunus* genus; you will only know which fruit you are growing by looking at the species part of the name. Once the full name has been given and there is no danger of confusion the genus is written as a letter (*J. regia*).

The species are then usually further subdivided into cultivars, usually varieties that have been cultivated by man. These are written with capitals and in inverted commas (*J. regia* 'Broadview'). You may find plants simply labelled with their common name but it is worth seeking out specific cultivars as these will give you particular refinements such as frost hardiness, disease resistance or an especially tasty harvest.

The number of trees you plant will be governed by your personal preferences and the amount of space you have, but bear in mind that you may need to plant more than one of each species to get a decent harvest. For fertilization to occur and the tree to grow fruit, the right pollen needs to get from the male to the female flowers. Some species of almond, sweet chestnut and walnut are self-fertile but many nut trees need fertilizing with pollen from one or more different cultivars of the same species. Even if you plant self-fertile cultivars you will probably get a better crop if you plant two or more compatible plants. Both trees need to be in flower at the same time; this may sound obvious but it can be a problem with hazels, where mild winters can cause the male catkins to flower and fade before the female flowers have even thought of opening. On some trees the pollen is transferred by the wind, with others bees and insects do the job inadvertently as they travel from flower to flower. Before you start planting it is worth checking the surrounding area, as you may find your neighbour has the perfect tree just over the fence or that a suitable specimen is lurking in your hedge. For easy cross-pollination, trees should be within a clear 18 m / 60 feet of each other, and remember buildings and other trees may block the pollen's path. For many species, elaborate pollination tables exist but the easiest way is simply to ask at the nursery where you buy the plants. They will also know the cultivars that will do best in your particular area.

Buying Plants

It is worth buying from a specialist nursery as with trees you really want to know exactly which cultivar you are buying. They will come either as bare-rooted or container-grown plants. Bare-rooted plants are sold or sent out when the plants are dormant, any time from late autumn to early spring. They need to be soaked in water for half an hour as soon as you get them and then planted as soon as possible so that they do not dry out. Container-grown plants can be bought at any time of year, but all nut trees are best planted in autumn or early winter, when the soil is not too cold or wet. If buying container-grown plants make sure that the plant is not pot-bound. When this occurs the roots run out of space and grow in tight circles following the contours of the pot. You can loosen them but it is better to start with straight roots which will grow directly into the surrounding soil.

Most will be one- or two-year old maidens consisting of a single upright stem with possibly a few side shoots. If you want to fan-train a tree it is much easier (and quicker) to buy a plant that is already formatively trained.

Many trees will come as grafted specimens rather than simple saplings. In most cases this is a better choice even though grafted trees tend to be more expensive. With a grafted tree a particular cultivar is grown on a specific rootstock ensuring you can pretty well guarantee the characteristics and eventual size of the plant. A seedling is grown from a seed (obviously) which had two parents and may not grow exactly like either of them. Grafted trees also tend to fruit more quickly, typically after four or five years, rather than ten or more. So, to summarize, if you have lots of space, lots of patience and like a gamble, go for a seedling, otherwise choose a grafted tree.

Tempting as it may be to buy a fully grown tree, these are not usually the best option, even if you can afford them. Young trees (one or two years old) settle in much better and will grow into stronger, healthier plants. In most cases they will also grow more quickly and will overtake a larger specimen in a few years.

Planting

When planning where to plant your trees make sure you allow sufficient space; 6 m / 20 feet may seem like a huge distance between two spindly young trees, it will not seem like that in ten years' time when they have matured and spread. Work out the final spread of the trees and allow a few feet extra between each one. This amount of space means the air circulates properly and your trees will be healthier. It also looks better.

Prepare the soil well, digging in compost, well-rotted manure or grit as necessary beforehand. Choose a day when the soil is not waterlogged or frozen. Planting in autumn or early winter ensures the soil is not too cold and gives the plant time to settle in before it has to worry about putting on new growth in the spring.

The hole must be large enough to accommodate the roots easily. The roots of bare-rooted plants should sit comfortably within the space. Most trees do not like being disturbed and will not take it kindly if their long taproots are bent or squashed in any way. The roots of container-grown plants should be gently teased out from the rootball so that they grow into the surrounding soil and do not just grow round in circles following the line of the original pot. All trees benefit from the addition of mycorrhizal fungi when planted. This is a natural fungus, which is available as a powder and allows the plant to take up nutrients from the soil more easily. The plant will slowly develop its own mycorrhizae, but by adding some at the beginning you will give the plant a hugely increased chance of settling in and thriving. Always follow the instructions on the packet.

Staking, Watering and Mulching

Unless they are in a very sheltered spot most trees will need staking for the first few years. Fix a stake so it will be on the windward side of the trunk. Container-grown plants need an angled stake so you do not disturb the root ball. It should form an angle of 45 degrees with the ground on the windward side. Fix the tree to the stake using tree ties or soft twine which will not damage the tree as it grows. Stakes can usually be removed after a couple of years. Shake the tree gently to check if the roots are firm. Always remove stakes at the start of the growing season to give the tree time to adjust while the weather is mild.

For the first year you should be prepared to water new trees once a week. Most need 5 cm / 2 inches rain per week, which equates to 23 litres / 5 gallons for a small tree and 46 litres / 10 gallons for a larger specimen. Trees should be mulched when planted but otherwise not fed for the first year. A layer of mulch will suppress weeds, reduce water evaporation and, depending what you use, gradually improve the soil. Ideally use organic matter such as garden compost or well-rotted manure and spread in a 5 cm / 2 inch deep circle round the tree, leaving a gap around the trunk to stop it rotting.

Harvesting

Autumn is the season of nut harvests. Some (almonds and walnuts) can be partially picked in the summer while still soft but the true harvest of fully ripe nuts takes place in the autumn. Most are better collected from the ground rather than picked from the trees. This ensures they are properly ripe and is also easier if you are dealing with a tall tree. If you have a lot of nut trees a Nut Wizard can be a huge help. This is basically a broom handle with a wire basket attached at one end. As you roll it along the ground it will magically pick up the nuts for you. They come in different sizes and somehow, completely brilliantly, they don't pick up that many leaves.

Problems

In comparison with fruit and vegetables most nut trees are remarkably pest free. The main problems you will encounter will be squirrel-related. They have clearly not heeded Cicely Mary Barker's poem *The Song of the Hazel-nut Fairy* where she says:

I will tell the squirrel,
'Here's a store for you;
But, kind sir, remember
The Nuthatch likes them too'.

Red squirrels are charming little creatures with delightfully tufted ears and dainty eating habits. Grey ones are thieving opportunists who will steal your entire crop given half a chance. Part of the problem is that the grey ones will take the nuts before they are ripe. One day your hazel will be laden with nuts, ready to pick in a week or so; the next day they will all have vanished. This is infuriating for humans and potentially damaging for the trees; nuts are their seeds and hope for the future and need to be fully ripe before they can be of any use. It is also one of the reasons why grey squirrels dominate over red ones, who wait nicely for the nuts to ripen before taking what they need.

There are some measures you can take. Isolated trees can be protected by a squirrel guard. This is a smooth tube of metal or plastic which fits round the trunk and prevents the squirrels climbing into the tree, a sort of fairground greasy pole. For these to be effective there needs to be a clear 3 m / 10 feet round the tree – the distance most squirrels can jump. Commercial deterrents are available based on capsaicin (the hot part of chillies) but they only last for a couple of weeks and even less if it rains. Moth balls, realistic toy snakes and onions will repel squirrels, but these don't look that good hanging in your trees. Fast dogs can also act as a deterrent. Whippets are the recommended breed but a friend's Border terrier put on a spectacular turn of speed and caught one, rather surprising everyone. What you do with the resultant corpse is up to you; Fergus Henderson has some excellent suggestions in his essential cookbook *Nose to Tail Eating*.

Many trees will need protection when young from rabbits and mice who nibble the bark. Guards made of chicken wire should be fixed round the tree, allowing plenty of room for growth. To give full protection the wire needs to extend 45 cm / 18 inches above the ground and be buried 15 cm / 6 inches below.

Deer can be a terrible problem but with them you need to protect the entire garden rather than individual specimens. A 2.5 m / 8 feet high fence should deter all but the most athletic jumpers.

Boring insects and weevils can cause holes in shells and empty cases but rarely do enough damage to worry about.

In some areas with hot summers the young trunks can risk being scalded by the sun. Paint them with a white latex paint diluted with 50% water.

Pruning

It is worth pruning most nut trees while young so they grow into a well-balanced shape; for most an open goblet is ideal. Specific advice is given within the sections but as a general rule you should prune the trees so the branches grow outwards and the centre remains light and airy. Cutting back one third of the central stem or leader in the first year will encourage stronger growth and more side shoots.

On grafted trees any suckers growing up from the base should be removed as these will be from the rootstock rather than the tree itself.

Once nut trees are established they don't need much pruning beyond the removal of the 'three Ds' (dead, diseased and damaged branches). This is particularly important with larger trees such as walnuts that develop heavy branches. Hazels and sweet chestnuts can be regularly coppiced, which is covered on page 74. Most nuts bear their flowers and fruit on new wood (tip-bearers) so if you regularly cut back the new growth you will reduce your chances of a good harvest.

Propagating

You can grow most nut trees from seed but seedlings can take at least 10-12 years to fruit and some never fruit at all. As they do not necessarily come true you cannot determine the quality of the nut until it is too late.

However it is fun to watch a little tree slowly emerging from a nut. Hazels, sweet chestnuts and oaks can all be successfully grown from seed as long as you give them a period of cold (stratification) which will ensure that the seed germinates in spring. Basically this involves mimicking the conditions that the nut would receive lying where it fell from the tree. Sow nuts in the autumn in individual pots of moist, well-drained compost. Bury the nut 5 cm / 2 inches deep and leave in a sheltered spot outside or in a cold frame over winter. To prevent mice and squirrels digging them up, cover the pots with chicken wire or keep the cold frames closed. The nuts should germinate the following spring. You can also stratify nuts in the fridge. Put them in a plastic bag with sphagnum moss and store in the salad drawer over winter. Plant out in spring.

Most nut trees have long taproots which are easily damaged. To prevent this, plant out the tree in its final place as soon as it develops a proper stem and leaves. You will almost certainly need to provide a circle of chicken wire to protect the little plant, enlarging it as the tree grows. Remember to allow enough space; your tiny 2 inch seedling may one day grow into a huge tree.

WILDLIFE IN THE GARDEN

Nut trees will encourage wildlife into your garden, both to live in the trees and to steal from your harvest. Some foragers such as birds, unlike grey squirrels, are a bonus in any garden. If you provide food for them on a regular basis they may even learn to go to the bird table for breakfast rather than your nut trees. The important thing is to provide food (and water) throughout the year, especially during winter when the birds who remain may find life hard.

Fat-based foods are excellent sources of nutrition for all birds and are easy to make. You should use lard or suet, which will remain solid, rather than butter, oil or left-over cooking fat which could get onto the birds' feathers.

You can use anything for a mould but yoghurt pots are a good size and are easy to remove once the fat has set. Make a hole in each side of the pot and thread a length of twine through to form the hanger.

Melt the fat and pour it over a bowl of mixed nuts, seeds and dried fruit. The best ratio is one part fat to two parts food. Almonds, hazelnuts, walnuts, peanuts and pecans are particularly nutritious.

You can also use wild bird seed, raw oats, bread crumbs and cheese; different mixes will attract different species of birds. Mix well, pour into the pots and leave overnight in the fridge to set. Cut away the plastic mould and hang the fat ball on your bird table or from a tree, anywhere that is out of reach of the dreaded squirrels!

Depending where you live you may also attract badgers, beavers, wild boar and dormice. You may not want the larger animals tramping through your garden but dormice are one of nature's charmers. Also known as the hazel dormouse they declined dramatically when the area of hazel plats in Kent decreased. Simply by planting hazels you will provide them with food and shelter.

ALMONDS

Almond trees are reasonably small, dainty trees with beautiful early spring blossom. Many of the ornamental cultivars do not produce good crops of nuts but, by choosing carefully, you can have spring flowers and nuts. Most grow to between 3-10 m / 10-33 feet and live between 30 and 50 years, although some have been known to live to over a hundred. Almond trees belong to the rose family and are closely related to cherries, plums and peaches. Strictly speaking, the fruits are drupes rather than nuts.

There are two main types of nut-producing almonds: *Prunus dulcis* which produce dessert almonds and *P. dulcis* var. *amara* which produce bitter-tasting nuts that are used for oil and flavourings. The bitterness is a useful warning as the nuts contain poisonous prussic acid. If eating nuts from an unknown tree, always nibble cautiously at first. Dessert almonds usually have white blossom, while that of the bitter nut trees is usually pink, supposedly deepening in colour with the level of bitterness.

Position

Almonds have a reputation of being tender but the trees are surprisingly tough; they flower early and it is both the blossom and the young nuts which are at risk from frosts. Some commercial growers use orchard heaters if frost is threatened but this is not a practical option for most gardeners. If the trees are small you can cover them with horticultural fleece on evenings when a frost is forecast. Ideally plant the trees against a south-facing wall which should give them sufficient protection. They like a sunny spot and are tolerant of heat in summer but don't like humidity. They are fully hardy and will grow in USDA zones 6-7.

Almonds will survive happily enough on poor soil but they will do much better in deep rich soil which is moisture-retentive and well-drained. They can survive drought conditions reasonably well but you won't get such a good harvest.

It is possible to grow the trees under glass, but you will need a large greenhouse and will get smaller crops as the trees need a cold dormant period in winter. Peach leaf curl is avoided but you run the risk of red spider mite and will almost certainly have to pollinate the flowers by hand.

Planting and Care

Unless your soil is the perfect crumbly loam that none of us have, add organic matter before planting and dig it in well. Follow the general planting instructions on page 62 and provide a stake as support for the first few years.

You should allow 3-6 m / 10-20 feet between trees, depending on the cultivars. Do not plant your almond trees near peaches as they could cross-pollinate and this can result in bitter and inedible nuts. Ideally plant them in different parts of the garden or on opposite sides of a barrier such as a hedge, wall or building.

As with most nut trees you are better with a grafted tree rather than a seedling. They will grow into a predetermined cultivar and should crop within 3-4 years. Most almonds are grafted onto plum rootstocks ('St Julian A' or 'Myran' will give you a tree 5-6 m / 15-20 feet tall). Dwarf trees are available on Pixy rootstock. They will reach 4 m / 13 feet and can be grown in containers but need regular watering throughout their lives. Plum rootstocks tolerate wetter soils and are fully hardy. Many of the best cultivars are specially-bred peach-almond crosses; these avoid the bitterness possible from cross-pollination mentioned above, tend to blossom later and crop well. Some cultivars are self-fertile but you will get a better crop with two or more compatible trees. The trees won't necessarily crop heavily every year; expect a good harvest every second or third.

As almonds blossom so early there is a risk that there won't be many insects to pollinate the flowers. One solution, if you have the space and inclination, is to have bee hives near the trees. It is possible to 'import' bees for the pollination period but this is not always ideal. In California millions of hives were transported every year, but this exposed the bees to a greatly increased risk of disease and in the last forty years the bee population is thought to have declined by half, due in part to this system. If the trees are small enough you can hand pollinate, transferring the pollen from the flowers using a soft paint brush.

In spring, once the soil has warmed up, mulch with garden compost or well-rotted manure, leaving a space round the trunk so it does not risk rotting. Alternatively you can give a general liquid feed. This is all the attention your tree should need.

Harvesting and Storing

Growing your own almonds enables you to have two harvests: the ripe autumn nuts and also the earlier green ones which are almost impossible to buy. In late spring or early summer, before the shell forms, you can enjoy the luxury of green almonds. They don't taste particularly almondy but are soft and delicious. Very early on you can eat them whole, later remove the shell and eat the pale creamy nut dipped in salt.

The nuts will ripen in mid autumn; you can tell when they are ready as the husks split open and the stalks begin to shrivel. At this point the fruits look rather like small peaches. The easiest way to collect them is to spread a sheet beneath the tree and give it a gentle shake. They won't ripen all at once, don't be tempted to pick the nuts, simply wait a few days and try again.

Remove the outer husks, lay out to dry in the sun for a few days and then store in a rodent-proof shed.

PRUNING AND TRAINING

You should prune in mid summer, as pruning in the damp of winter is more likely to encourage fungal disease and canker. With young trees you should aim to create an open goblet shape by removing crossing branches and thinning side shoots back to an outward-facing bud. You can control the height by cutting back the leader (the main upward-growing stem). Almonds fruit on one-year old wood so prune back some branches which fruited the previous year. Once the trees are fully grown you should only need to remove the 'three Ds' and any badly crossing stems.

Almonds can be trained against a wall, which provides protection and gives a beautiful display of blossom. They are best as fans; attach wires or canes to the wall, radiating out from the base of the tree. Ideally choose a tree with two or three strong side shoots and tie them gently to the supports. As new shoots grow you will be able to fill in any gaps. Prune in early summer, cutting away any unwanted stems. The side shoots off the main stems will carry the fruit so only cut them away if they are congested or inward-facing.

PROBLEMS

Squirrels will probably be your greatest problem. You can deal with them in any of the ways suggested on page 64.

The trees are prone to leaf curl. This causes blisters on the leaves which become distorted, turn red and may drop early. It is mostly caused by damp weather in spring. It is obviously not practical to stand over your tree with an umbrella but it can help to move container-grown pots under cover. Many cultivars, including most of the peach-almond hybrids have some level of resistance.

Slugs and snails often eat the leaves on young trees. Plants in containers can be protected by a ring of copper tape round the pot; otherwise saucers of beer will give you happily drunken corpses, or a surrounding circle of grit will act as a deterrent.

A Selection of Almond Cultivars
(*Prunus dulcis*)

P. d. '**Ingrid**': This is a peach-almond hybrid from Sweden. It has large pink flowers, is self-fertile and has some resistance to peach leaf curl.

P. d. '**Mandaline**': This cultivar flowers in mid to late spring which means that the pretty pink blossom is less at risk from frost. It is self-fertile, has good resistance to fungal disease and crops well.

P. d. '**Robijn**': This is a similar cultivar to 'Ingrid' from Holland.

P. d. '**Titan**': These trees are hardy and late flowering. They are resistant to peach leaf curl and produce sweet, thin-shelled nuts. They are not completely self-fertile.

HAZELS AND HAZELNUTS

Hazels are everything you could want in a nut tree. They grow to a reasonable size, rarely reaching more than 4-6 m / 13-20 feet tall, they have pretty catkins in spring, you can coppice them, controlling the size even more and earning yourself a supply of useful stakes and, if you can beat the squirrels, you will have a harvest of delicious nuts. The commercially packaged nuts have lost much of their allure by being available year round; the ones you grow in your garden will taste a thousand times better than anything you can buy and will convince you of the tree's desirability.

The term hazel generally covers any plant in the *Corylus* genus. Cobnut is the English name for *C. avellana,* which are the true hazels and filbert refers to *C. maxima.* Filberts are longer nuts which are fully encased in their husks. Cobnuts are rounder, with a husk that partially encases the nut and resembles a frilly bonnet. This would seem clear but the names are set to trap the unwary; 'Lambert's Filbert', dating from the early nineteenth century, is also called the Kentish Cob. In practice, cobs and filberts interbreed merrily and it is easier to refer to them generally as hazels. Unless specified, we have use 'hazel' to cover both cobnuts and filberts.

Position

Hazels like a sunny site but will grow perfectly well in the dappled shade of the woodland where they are naturally found. They will grow well in most soils as long as they are not waterlogged. They fruit best on poor stony land; rich fertile soil encourages leafy growth instead. They are fully hardy and will thrive in USDA zone 7.

Planting and Care

Most hazels should fruit within 4-6 years. Many are partly self-fertile but will produce a better crop if cross-pollinated with a compatible cultivar.

As a rough guide they should be planted 6 m / 20 feet apart for trees, 3 m / 10 feet for hedges. A nut walk works well if it is 4 m / 13 feet wide with two staggered rows of hazels on either side 3 m / 10 feet apart and with 1.2 m / 4 feet between the rows. This is the plan Gertrude Jekyll used at Munstead Wood and allows the back rows of trees to show in between the front ones. Eventually the trees will arch over the path and meet in the middle.

You can either buy bare-rooted plants or container-grown plants. Hazels do not have a deep taproot like many nuts and therefore do not mind being transplanted. Check that container-grown plants are not pot-bound; if the roots are twisting round inside the pot the plant will not settle so well in the ground. If you can, it is best to buy a plant with several stems. If there is a particularly strong leader or central stem cut it back by about half. This will encourage the plant to branch out into the open goblet shape you want. Stake the young plants for 2-3 years unless the site is very sheltered. Water regularly for the first year following the instructions on page 62. Mulch the trees in early winter or spring with garden compost or well-rotted manure.

Each tree has male and female catkins. The yellow male catkins appear in late winter before the leaves and light up the garden. They are one of the joyous signs that spring is on the way. The females are like a bud with tufty red styles. On a fine dry day, play Cupid and tap the branches with a stick to encourage the pollen from the male flowers to waft onto the female flowers. Pollination can be poor in a wet spring and following warm winters the male flowers may emerge early and wither before the female flowers open. In this case, save as much pollen as you can in a paper bag and scatter it when the female flowers open.

Harvesting and Storing

To beat the squirrels, you may need to pick your nuts in late summer and eat them straight away. For nuts that will store well you need to wait until they are fully ripened in early autumn. To store, spread the nuts out to dry in a warm place, turning every few days. Remove the husks and put the nuts in a paper bag somewhere cool and rodent-free such as a larder, outdoor store or fridge. The nuts will keep perfectly till Christmas and probably long after.

Pruning for Nuts

Prune all hazels in mid to late winter. The best shape for a good harvest is a goblet on a single stem. This allows light and air to circulate through the tree. You want six to ten main stems branching out from the main trunk, roughly 30-45 cm / 12-18 inches above the ground. In winter cut away the 'three Ds' and any crossing branches. Also remove the tall vertical shoots that grow up through the middle of the plant heading straight for the sky. Most nuts grow on one-year old stems and spurs. Remove some of the older wood to encourage new growth. Dig up any suckers and, if wanted, plant them up to increase your stock (see propagating, below).

If your trees are planted on rich soil you may find you get leafy growth rather than flowers and fruit. To correct this you should 'brut' the trees. In late summer bend back some of the new shoots halfway along their length, snapping the stem but not completely breaking it off. Leave it in place. This will prevent too much new growth and will also encourage flower buds to develop in the autumn. When you prune in winter the broken stems can be cut back to 10-12 cm/ 4-5 inches.

Pruning for a Nut Walk

Assuming you want the stems to arch over the path you should cut back any outward growing branches in favour of the more upright ones. It is up to you whether you coppice back to a stool or leave a single trunk.

Coppicing

A particular type of pruning that works well with hazels (and sweet chestnuts) is coppicing. Bronze Age Britons discovered that deciduous trees responded well to being cut back to their base and would send up new growth the following spring. The constant regeneration does the tree no harm and actually extends its lifespan. Hazels are fast growing and respond well to being coppiced. They can be cut back every seven to fifteen years but remember this will reduce your nut crop. The thinner branches make good pea sticks while the thicker stems make excellent bean poles, fence posts and firewood, once seasoned.

Coppicing is a healthy option for the general area as it regularly allows light to reach the woodland floor. Wild flowers which have lain dormant for years will provide a brilliant carpet for a few years while the stems grow back and then fade again as the canopy thickens and cuts out the light. This regeneration is good for the plants, wildlife and soil. Two or three hazels will give you an ever-changing wild garden and a constant supply of stakes and pea sticks.

Coppicing should be carried out in winter when the plant is dormant. A young tree with a single stem should be cut to 15-10 cm / 6-12 inches above ground. The following spring a number of new shoots will grow up. These can be cut in seven to ten years just above the original stool or stump and so the process is repeated, again and again. If you want to stagger the cutting you can cut one third of the stems after 4-5 years. Cut another third each of the following two years and then leave for seven years. This method does not bring about the complete regeneration of the forest floor but it has the advantage of keeping your coppice looking bushy.

Propagating

Hazels do not necessarily come true from seed but as all are edible and grow to a similar size this isn't a great problem. Plant the seed in a pot following the instructions on page 72 and pot on a couple of times before planting out. A much quicker way to acquire new plants is to dig up any suckers in autumn and either pot them up or plant them *in situ*. You can also increase your stock by layering. Choose a stem which is near the ground and in autumn bury a length midway along, holding it in place with a peg. The following autumn the buried stem will have formed roots and can be cut away from the parent plant.

Problems

Grey squirrels are the pest above all others. See page 64 for eradication methods.

Nut weevils will bury into some nuts but are not usually enough of a problem to worry about.

A Selection of Hazels (*Corylus* spp.)

Cobnuts and filberts interbreed promiscuously and wherever there are two or three hazels gathered together you will find a great variety of seedlings.

C. americana: This is a fully hardy species.

C. maxima 'Purpurea': This cultivar has deep purple leaves and purple-tinged catkins. The husks round the nuts are also purply. It grows 6x5 m / 20x16 ft.

C. avellana 'Purpurea': This is a less common cultivar than the one above but is a much prettier plant. it is less dense and the light filters through the leaves as if through rubies.

C. a. 'Butler': This was a chance find on Mr Butler's plantation in Oregon in the 1950s. It crops well, with an attractive round nut but has slightly less flavour than the 'Kentish Cob'.

C. a. 'Gunslebert': This is a vigorous cultivar with large nuts which ripen in early to mid autumn.

C. a. 'Lambert's Filbert' or 'Kentish cob': This bears well-flavoured nuts which ripen in late summer or early autumn.

C. avellana 'Contorta', the corkscrew hazel: This is a popular ornamental plant with madly twisting branches. It also produces good nuts. It is usually grafted onto ordinary hazel rootstock so remove any suckers as they will grow straight.

SWEET CHESTNUTS

Sweet chestnuts can be grown as coppiced trees or individual parkland specimens. They came to Britain with the Romans and are now naturalized, with 44 million growing in the country. They can reach 30-36 m / 100-120 feet and live for 250 years, with coppiced trees reaching over 350-400 years with a girth of 12-15 m / 40-50 feet.

These are not trees for the impatient though; most don't start fruiting until they are 25-30 years old. However, they are one of the most beautiful trees you can grow. The lower branches spread out horizontally, while the upper ones grow vertically, creating a pyramid shape. Capability Brown used them extensively in the eighteenth century and they are a common sight on English parkland, providing shade for the grazing sheep below.

The bark starts smooth and silvery, developing deep ridges which curve round the trunk as the tree ages. It is not known why these ridges develop; they follow the lines of the sap-connecting tissues and can be diagonal in either direction while the grain of the wood below remains vertical.

The long, elliptical leaves are dark and glossy with pale, slightly furry undersides. The flowers appear in mid summer. The creamy catkins smell rather sickly but it is thought that the smell attracts pollinating insects. Gradually throughout the summer the female flowers at the base of each catkin transforms into the nuts in their spiny green cases. By autumn the trees are covered with lime green Christmas baubles.

Coppiced sweet chestnuts form much larger plants than hazels. They grow quickly and within fifteen years they will produce 9 m /

30 feet poles 8-10 cm / 3-4 inches thick. Each time the tree is cut back it regrows with youthful vigour, thinking that it has not yet reached maturity. The wood is hard, lasts well in the soil and splits straight, making it ideal for fence posts. Traditionally the wood was used for barrel staves, coffins and underground pipes. The poles were also used to support hops, with two thousand being used for every acre of hops. Much less attractively these are now largely supported by wire. During the Second World War coppiced sweet chestnuts were used to make over 1,500 miles of tank tracks on the Normandy beaches.

Position

Sweet chestnuts like full sun; they are parkland trees and like space around them (probably to show off their gracious shape). They do best on well-drained, slightly acidic soil. Rhododendrons and azaleas are good indicators of suitable conditions. They are fully hardy and grow best in USDA zones 6-7.

Planting and Care

They are rarely self-fertile and you usually need at least two compatible cultivars to get a good crop of nuts. Some cultivars, such as 'Marigoule' are partially self-fertile but will always produce a better harvest with another tree nearby.

However small the trees are that you buy, you should allow at least 8 m / 26 feet between coppiced trees, more between individual trees which will easily reach 20 m / 65 feet x 15 m / 50 feet.

Harvesting and Storing

The nuts put on most of their growth in early autumn so make sure that the soil does not dry out during this time. Ripe nuts fall at the same time as the leaves. If you have several trees a Nut Wizard can be a huge help (see page 63). The harvesting period will last for a couple of weeks and you need to collect the nuts every few days as they deteriorate quickly on damp ground. You also need to remove the prickly cases; the easiest way to do this is to roll them along the ground with a booted foot.

Fresh nuts have a high water content and do not store well. Drying them in the sun or indoors at room temperature will turn the sugar to starch and keep them preserved. You can then put them in paper bags in the fridge, where they will keep for several weeks.

PRUNING AND TRAINING

You should prune young trees so they form an open goblet shape, cutting the branches back to an outward-facing bud. Within a few years, the tree will be so large that you don't need to worry about shaping individual branches and simply need to keep an eye out for the 'three Ds'.

To coppice the trees you should follow the method for hazels on page 74. Sweet chestnuts will form much larger coppices and can be cut back every ten years or so. Bear in mind that the trees will not produce nuts so readily if coppiced.

PROBLEMS

The American chestnut (*C. dentata*) had been a vital source of food and timber for both the Native Americans and the early settlers. In the early 1900s chestnut blight, which causes cankers on the bark, destroyed nearly every tree. It was very contagious, being carried by the wind and birds, and spread literally like wildfire. Japanese (*C. crenata*) and Chinese (*C. mollissima*) species are resistant and it is hybrids of these trees you will now mostly find in North America.

Otherwise sweet chestnuts are largely problem free. Chestnut weevil and chestnut coddling moth can cause problems boring through the shells and eating the kernels. You can use sticky or pheromone traps but there are usually enough nuts for everyone.

A Selection of Sweet Chestnuts (*Castanea* spp.)

Sweet or Spanish chestnut (*C. sativa*): This forms a broad tree with widely-spreading branches and good fruits.

***C. s.* 'Albomarginata'**: The leaves are edged creamy-white.

***C. s.* 'Asplenifolia'**: The leaves are deeply cut

***C. s.* 'Marron de Lyon'**: Grown for its fruits.

Chinese chestnut (*C. mollissima*): This forms a rounder tree than the sweet or Spanish chestnut. It is grown widely in North America.

WALNUTS

Walnuts are large stately trees, originating in the Caucasus Mountains of Central Asia. They can live for hundreds of years, reaching 30 m / 100 feet tall with a spread of 15-20 m / 50-70 feet. *Juglans regia* is the common, Persian or English walnut which was introduced to Britain by the Romans. *J. nigra* or the black walnut is an American species which grows faster but needs well-drained soil and warmth to do well.

They have large, shiny aromatic leaves. The male catkins are a greenish yellow and the female flowers appear in groups of three looking like little red stars; in some species these can be at risk from frost.

These are trees for the future as much as the present, the seventeenth century proverb 'walnuts and pears you plant for your heirs' was right.

Position

Walnuts need a sunny site that is well-protected from frost. Ideally they like a well-drained, moisture-retentive soil with a neutral pH. On light soils which dry out in summer the fruits can drop before they are fully ripe. They are fully hardy and are best in USDA zones 4-5.

PLANTING AND CARE

When planting a walnut you also have to consider the surrounding plants. Walnuts produce a chemical called juglone which impedes the growth of many plants and can kill apple and pear trees. Grass, bulbs and most perennials are unaffected and although juglone is present in the nuts it is harmless to humans. It also occurs in the leaves but they can be safely composted. It is a clever evolutionary development to ensure that the trees don't have too much competition.

Choose a grafted cultivar which will fruit after 4-5 years, rather than a seedling which could take fifteen to twenty. They have the added advantage of being more frost-resistant.

You should allow a minimum of 10 m / 30 feet between trees, 12-15 m / 36-50 feet is better. Dig a deep hole which will easily accommodate the rootball. If your garden is on clay you should incorporate plenty of grit and organic matter into the planting hole and surrounding soil.

You may need to guard the young tree against rabbits (see page 64). Stake for the first couple of years until the tree has firmly established its roots. Feed annually in spring with a general-purpose fertilizer and mulch with garden compost or well-rotted manure. You should also be prepared to water for the first couple of years.

Some cultivars are self-fertile but the male and female flowers can bloom at different times making the tree non-productive. As with most self-fertile nut trees, you will get a better, more reliable harvest if you plant more than one tree.

HARVESTING AND STORING

Botanically speaking, walnuts are a green drupe with a wrinkled seed. As they ripen the outer husk turns dark brown and will come away from the stem easily when ripe. You will probably find that your walnut trees will only fruit well every 2 to 3 years. If you have your own trees you can also pick green walnuts in early to mid summer and make your own pickled walnuts (see page 108). Test a few nuts by spearing them with a thin knitting needle. It should go easily through the husk, if it doesn't it means that the nuts are already too hard and should be left to fully ripen. Traditionally the night of 24-25 July is the harvesting time in Italy where the nuts are used to make Nocino. These are perfect for pickling or, of course, making the liqueur. Harvesting some nuts early will allow the tree to concentrate on the remaining ones and should improve your autumn crop.

In autumn the husks will split open to reveal the ripe nuts. Shake or tap the branches (wearing a protective hat; a falling walnut can be quite painful). Remove the nuts from their husks immediately to avoid the risk of fungal disease. Wear waterproof or old gardening gloves to do this; the husks contain a powerful brown dye. Store the nuts in a cool, rodent-free place.

Wet walnuts are delicious eaten straight from the tree. If you want to store the nuts you will need to dry them. Wash and spread out to dry somewhere cool and dry. Leave for 2-3 days, turning them occasionally to ensure they dry evenly. The nuts will now keep for 6-12 months.

Pruning and Training

For the first few years, prune the trees in late summer to create an open goblet shape. Remove any low branches so you have a clear trunk of 1.8-2.5 m / 6-8 feet. This will allow for easier harvesting and should deter squirrels. Once the trees are established no pruning is necessary other than the removal of the 'three Ds', again in late summer.

Problems

Walnut blight can be a problem. Spotting appears on the leaves and if it spreads to the fruits they will blacken. It is usually caused by cool, wet weather at blossom time. Many cultivars now have a good level of resistance.

A Selection of Walnut Trees (*Juglans* spp.)

In cool areas such as Britain and much of North America it is essential to grow cultivars which come into leaf late and flower after any danger of frost.

Common, Persian or English walnut (*J. regia*): These tend to bear good fruit. When young, the leaves are an attractive purply-bronze colour.

J. r. '**Broadview**': Originally from British Columbia, this is a moderately vigorous tree with good harvests. It is partially self-fertile but more productive when cross-pollinated with a compatible cultivar.

J. r. '**Buccaneer**': This is a very vigorous Dutch cultivar, growing into an upright shape. It has good disease resistance and is self-fertile but has half the production levels of 'Broadview'.

J. r. '**Franquette**': This is an old French cultivar and grows into a large, spreading tree. It produces good nuts, comes into leaf late in the season and is not susceptible to frost but can be slow to bear fruit. It is partially self-fertile but crops better when cross pollinated.

J. r. '**Northdown Clawnut**': A medium-sized tree, this is partially self-fertile and bears large nuts.

J. r. '**Rita**': This small cultivar reaches 8 m / 25 feet making it suitable for smaller gardens. It is reasonably reliably self-fertile.

J. cinerea (**Butternut**): The trees are fully hardy but the flowers can be damaged by late frosts.

J. nigra (**American or black walnut**): The nuts have a thick shell and a rich smoky flavour. The trees are hardy and much prized for their wood.

J. manchuria (**Manchurian walnut**): These are tough trees and although they like warmth they are less susceptible to frost damage.

HICKORIES AND PECANS

In nut terms, pecans are the royalty of hickories but all the trees are attractive and, if you have the space, are certainly worth growing just for their looks. Most have good autumn colour and some have ornamental bark. Getting a good harvest is a bit of a gamble but becoming more realistic with the development of new cultivars. They were traditionally grown in the southern states of North America but breeding programmes have now extended the potential areas. Northern, western and eastern pecans all have distinct characteristics and levels of hardiness. The northern ones have a good frost resistance and the nuts do not need such long summers to ripen; these are the trees to grow in northern Europe and the cooler states of North America. These are long-lived, large trees when grown in warm climates, surviving four to five hundred years and reaching 30 m / 100 feet. In temperate regions they often only reach a third of this size.

Position

Above all, pecans need sun and a deep, well-drained soil, with a reliable supply of water. Pecan wood is brittle so avoid windy sites, even harvesting roughly can damage branches. All hickories are hardy, best suited to USDA zones 5-6.

Like walnuts, hickories can produce juglone, a chemical which harms some plants, in particular apples and pears; do not plant them adjacent to each other.

Planting and Care

They grow male and female catkins on the same tree but self-pollination is not totally reliable; you are assured a better harvest with two or three compatible trees. Plant at least 10 m / 30 feet apart.

They have long taproots, follow the general planting instructions on page 62 but take extra care not to damage the root.

The trees spend the first 3-4 years establishing their roots so during this time keep them well-watered and the surrounding ground clear of competitive weeds. Don't worry if they don't seem to be growing much at this point, they will be settling into their new home.

Harvesting and Storing

The nuts grow in clusters, the husk starting green and then turning brown and eventually splitting when ripe. They will be ready to harvest from mid autumn through to mid winter depending on the variety and how well the nuts have been able to ripen over summer. Once the nuts start to split you should spread a sheet on the ground and give the tree a good shake.

The nuts are better if dried; spread them out on paper in a cool dry place and leave for a couple of weeks. At this point they should snap rather than bend. They can absorb strong smells so do not store them near crops such as onions. Once dried they will keep in a paper bag in the fridge for at least six months or for well over a year if frozen.

Pruning and Training

Hickories don't need much pruning; simply remove the 'three Ds' and any crossing stems. Sometimes in summer, branches can break for no apparent reason; it is worth shortening the longest to prevent this.

Problems

In areas of high humidity pecans can develop scab but there are now resistant cultivars available. Regular watering will reduce stress and keep the trees resistant to most other diseases.

A Selection of Hickories (*Carya* spp.)

Pecan (*C. illinoinensis*): These are rounded trees with attractive grey bark. They spread to 20 m / 70 feet so give them plenty of room when planting. They will only tolerate a few days below -12°C / 10 F. The northern cultivars divide into standard ('Colby', 'Kanza' and 'Major'), very early ('Devore', 'Fisher' and 'Gibson') and ultra early ('Deerstand' and 'Green Island Beaver'). Ask your local nursery which is the most suitable for your area.

Shagbark hickory (*C. ovata*): These have small nuts in a very tough shell, but they are good to eat. The trees are fully hardy and the leaves turn golden yellow in autumn.

Bitternut or swamp hickory (*C. cordiformis*): The name says it all; these nuts are thick-shelled and unpalatable. However the leaves do turn a brilliant yellow in autumn.

Hognut or pignut hickory (*C. glabra*): Again, these aren't worth growing for the nuts but the leaves turn yellow in autumn and the bark is beautiful; grey with deep furrows.

PISTACHIOS

Pistachios are not an obvious garden tree but if you can grow olives you could certainly try pistachios. Even if you get no nuts they are still lovely trees with attractive blossom and bark. They grow 8-10 m / 25-30 feet tall. The blossom appears in spring just before the leaves and the delicate pinky-white flowers are often interestingly tinged with pale green or even turquoise. The nuts need long hot summers to ripen which is why harvests in Northern Europe and the colder parts of North America can be erratic.

Position

These trees come from the Middle East and need a cold winter period as well as long hot summers. They will happily grow in areas of drought and on poor sandy soils but they do not like to be wet in winter. Like many Middle Eastern and Mediterranean plants it is the combination of cold and damp which does most harm. In temperate climates they do best if grown within the shelter of a south-facing wall. This minimizes the risk of frost damage to the blossom and maximizes any summer warmth. It is possible to grow pistachios in pots, although the trees require more care in terms of regular watering and feeding.

Planting and Care

As with all nuts, you are best buying grafted trees. These should start to crop after 3-4 years and will remain productive for about fifty. The male and female flowers grow on different trees; female flowers which are not fertilized grow into upsettingly hollow nuts. Commercial orchards usually allow one male plant for every 6-8 females.

Harvesting and Storing

The nuts grow in clusters like bunches of grapes. When they are ready to eat the shells split open, giving rise to the belief that the nuts are laughing. They are best stored in their shells.

Pruning and Training

Prune the trees in mid summer to create an open goblet shape. To wall train attach wires or canes to the wall, radiating out from the base of the tree. Ideally choose a tree with two or three strong side shoots and tie them gently to the supports. As new shoots grow you will be able to fill in any gaps.

Problems

Apart from their dislike of cold and damp, pistachios are remarkably trouble free. If you grow them under cover you may be troubled by red spider mite. These tiny sap-sucking insects weave fine webs over the plant and are ultimately very harmful but they can be controlled by biological methods.

A Selection of Pistachios (*Pistacia* spp.)

P. vera: This is the species to grow for a crop of nuts. They are less attractive than the Chinese species but they do hold the magical promise of a harvest.

Chinese pistachio (*P. chinensis*): This is a pretty species with aromatic red flowers and lovely autumn colour. It is hardier but it's not the one to grow if you want fruits as they are tiny. It is also large, reaching 15-25 m / 50-80 feet tall and 7-10 m / 22-30 feet wide.

OAKS AND ACORNS

These are not usually grown for their crops, although acorns were an important source of food as early as 5,000 BC and may, perhaps, have their day again. Their history, mythology, appearance and nobility all make oaks well worth growing. On top of this they provide habitats for myriad wildlife. There are about five hundred different species but for the best acorns you want to grow white oaks. Those of red oaks take two years to mature and tend to be very bitter.

Position

Oaks prefer clay soils but in practice they are remarkably unfussy. They like sunshine but will tolerate some shade and most cultivars are fully hardy (USDA zones 3-9). All in all, if you have the space, they are easy trees to grow.

Planting and Care

Oaks vary in size from 6-30 m / 20-100 feet in height, with corresponding variations in width. Check the final size of your tree and plan your planting distances accordingly. The trees are usually seedlings and will either be bare-rooted or container-grown; either way follow the planting instructions on page 62. Most oaks are not self-fertile; for a reliable harvest of acorns plant two or three compatible cultivars.

Harvesting and Storing

Some species can take over twenty years to produce a good crop so choose your trees carefully. Once they have started to produce fruit they usually crop well every 2-4 years. As the acorns ripen they change from green to brown and fall from the tree. At this stage they will come away from their cups easily and can be stored for several months as long as they are kept dry.

Before eating you need to leach the harmful tannins from the nuts. The best way to do this is to repeatedly boil the nuts in fresh water until it runs clear.

Pruning and Training

Oaks need no pruning other than to remove the 'three Ds' and any badly crossed branches. Any pruning is best done in late autumn or early spring as the flowers and fruits are formed on the current season's growth.

Problems

Most oaks are remarkably trouble free. They may be eaten by caterpillars and galls may be formed by gall wasps but these should not be a major problem.

Squirrels are, of course a pest; eating the acorns as well as burying them for future use. This may not help humans but many oak trees grow from forgotten squirrel caches of acorns.

A Selection of Oaks (*Quercus* spp.)

Common or English oak (*Q. robur*): These are the trees of English parkland, with their distinctively indented leaves, spreading branches and fissured bark. While the acorns are not especially delicious the looks of this majestic tree easily make up for its shortfall in the taste department.

Live oak (*Q. virginiana*): A native of south-eastern USA this species is not fully hardy but bears very pleasant-tasting nuts which are low in tannins.

Sweet or chinkapin oak (*Q. muehlenbergii*): This species is native to eastern North America and is reputed to bear the sweetest-tasting acorns.

BEECHES AND BEECH MAST

These are large, handsome trees whose nuts have been eaten since prehistoric times, although they are now mostly regarded as animal fodder. They have a stately upright habit and, when in leaf, cast a deep shade. The leaves are an attractive brilliant lime-green in spring, turning to equally attractive shades of rust and brown in autumn.

POSITION

Beeches do best on chalk and limestone but in practice, like oaks, they are remarkably unfussy. They are frost tolerant but do best in temperate climates with cool summers and mild winters (USDA zone 5).

PLANTING AND CARE

The trees like a deep, moist, well-drained soil which is slightly acidic. Plant following the general instructions on page 62, allowing sufficient space between the trees. For the first few years you should water and mulch regularly while the tree establishes its roots.

HARVESTING AND STORING

The spiny brown husks partially open in autumn when the nuts ripen. They can be collected as they fall, ideally before the local wildlife gets to them. The husks and inner skin need to be removed for the nuts to keep well.

PRUNING AND TRAINING

Apart from the removal of the 'three Ds' beech trees should not need pruning.

PROBLEMS

The trees have no real problems, and even squirrels don't usually make themselves a nuisance!

A SELECTION OF BEECH TREES (*Fagus* spp.)

European beech (*F. sylvatica*): These trees can take time to establish so be prepared to water and mulch for several years. There are a huge variety of cultivars with differing shapes and leaf colours; ask at your nursery for ones that will suit your requirements.

American beech (*F. grandiflora*): This species has sharply-toothed leaves which are dark green in summer turning golden brown in autumn. The kernels can be small.

PEANUTS

Peanuts are so easy to buy that it may scarcely seem worth growing them but, for interest alone, these plants are worth a space in any garden. They are annuals which form attractive pea-like plants 30-60 cm / 1-2 feet tall. Uniquely in the natural world their flowers grow a stem or peg after fertilization which grows down towards the ground and buries itself in the earth. It is here, underground, that the pod containing the nuts grows. They originated in South America but cultivars have been developed with short growing seasons which can be grown in more temperate climates.

Position

Peanuts need to be grown in full sun. The nuts may develop underground but the parent plant needs warmth while the nuts grow.

They like a moist, well-drained soil that is friable so the pods can easily develop. They can be successfully grown in a container as long as it is wide enough to accommodate the arching stems. As the pods only penetrate about 8 cm / 3 inches the containers can be shallow but should, ideally be about 1 m / 3 feet diameter. The pods need to be in the same soil as the mother plant.

They can also be grown successfully under glass, in containers or open beds.

PLANTING AND CARE

Unless they have been treated or processed, you can grow plants from any peanuts. The only disadvantage to this method is that you will not know which cultivar you are growing and may well end up with one that requires a long season and high temperatures. It is much safer to plant a particular cultivar.

Peanuts are not frost hardy so if you intend to grow them outside wait until any danger of cold weather has passed. Grow the seeds in small pots in spring. After about fourteen days, the seeds should germinate and can be potted on. Transplant to their final positions once the weather is warm, taking care not to damage the roots.

Each yellow flower lasts barely a day; they open in the morning and by evening they have withered, ready to start producing the nuts. The plants can tolerate drought and require little in the way of nutrients but will appreciate regular watering and the occasional feed of liquid seaweed. Do not water too much as harvesting time approaches as your crop may start to grow into new plants. Additional calcium can also help the seed set. As with all annual crops they should not be grown in the same place year after year. Peanuts are nitrogen fixers and can usefully form part of a general crop rotation.

HARVESTING AND STORING

The pods are ready to harvest when the leaves turn yellow, a sign that the nuts have taken all the goodness from the mother plant. The veins within the pods darken as the nuts ripen, with those nearest the plant ripening first. You should harvest when the soil is dry so the pods can easily be dug up and wiped clean. If you want to store the nuts you should dry them first, spreading them out somewhere warm and ideally, sunny. If the nuts are not thoroughly dried their oil can turn rancid and they can develop a carcinogenic fungus. Once dried, the nuts will keep well in the fridge or freezer.

A Selection of Peanut Cultivars (*Arachis hypogaea*)

The cultivars below all have a short growing season making them suitable for cooler, temperate climates.

'**Early Spanish**': These grow into neat compact plants and although the yields aren't huge, the nuts are sweet and well-flavoured.

'**Spanish**': This is a similar cultivar.

'**Valencia**': This cultivar is larger, reaching up to 1.3 m / 45 inches and has reddish stems and large leaves. It only needs a short growing season but fruits better if the season is warm.

NUTS IN THE KITCHEN

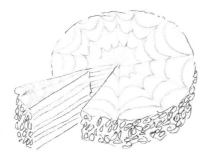

I follow recipes exactly - until I decide not to.

(Ina Garten)

GENERAL GUIDELINES TO USING OUR RECIPES

Our recipes give both metric and imperial measurements. For best results, please follow one or the other, do not mix and match within the recipe.

Unless otherwise specified in the recipe: eggs are always large, butter is always unsalted, dark (bittersweet) chocolate is minimum 70% cocoa solids, cup and spoon measurements are level.

You know your own oven best. We have found that all ovens vary and have their own idiosyncratic hot and cold spots. The best way to be sure is to use an oven thermometer rather than rely on the temperature gauge knob. In baking, use your own judgement and don't be afraid to cook for another 10 minutes or take something out of the oven a little early if it is not yet, or is already, golden brown or set to the recipe instructions.

Nuts are one of our favourite ingredients and endlessly versatile. You can sprinkle them in salads to add protein, add them to crumbles to provide body and crunch, use them to decorate cakes or grind them up to thicken stews. To ensure you get the best out of your nuts there are a few basic principles which will apply across the nut family.

HANDLING AND STORAGE TIPS

Buying and Storing Nuts

Nuts are high in oil. This makes them extremely good for you but also means that they can go off if not stored correctly. Buy in small quantities and keep in air tight containers in a cool dark place. Always buy from shops with high turnover.

Nuts freeze well and will keep up to two years in the freezer. This is particularly handy for seasonal nuts like cobnuts or chestnuts which you cannot always get year round.

It's up to you whether you buy nuts salted or unsalted. For baking of course you want unsalted but in many savoury dishes salted will work as well if that is what is more readily available. As a general rule, we prefer to buy unsalted as we like to control the flavour and level of seasoning ourselves.

Toasting Nuts

Toasting nuts is almost always worth it. It brings out the inherent nuttiness, deepens the golden colouring and crisps up the texture. Just heat the oven to 180°C / 350°F / Gas 4. Spread the nuts out on an oven tray and just pop them in the oven for ten minutes. If they are golden and nutty smelling, take them out. If not, give the tray a shake to spread them round a bit and pop them back in for another 3-5 minutes. Do keep an eye on them though; there is no coming back from a burnt nut. Cool completely before using.

You can also toast nuts in a dry frying pan (skillet) over a medium heat for a few minutes stirring constantly to prevent catching.

Technically speaking, you can freeze toasted nuts but we find it is better to freeze them 'raw' and toast up before using.

Nuts keep freshest in the shell but naturally you will have to remove that shell to eat them (unless of course you are Bond villain, Jaws). For culinary purposes, it is usually easiest to buy nuts ready shelled. We have broken a lot of finger nails shelling pistachios (and why is it those packets always contain at least half a dozen pesky little nuts closed tight as clam shells?). If shelled nuts are available and we are going to cook with them we often buy shelled. If you are eating the nut fresh or have been foraging you will need to shell them yourself, so here are some guidelines.,

For most nuts (cobnuts, walnuts etc.) you can just crack the hard outer shell with nut crackers or a meat mallet and peel off the outside shell. For almonds and hazelnuts you may also wish to remove the inner skin which surrounds the sweet white nut. The best way to do this is to spread the shelled nuts out on a baking tray (sheet) and bake in a 180°C / 350°F / Gas 4 oven. Bake for 15 minutes and then put into a clean tea towel, rub vigorously and the thin papery skin will simply come off.

Walnut and pecan nuts with skin on when combined with milk or cream can turn a purplish grey colour. This will still taste delicious but can look a little unappetising. They are not easy to peel. You can either roast as you would hazelnuts and rub in a tea towel or, more successfully, boil for three minutes, rub dry and if necessary toast in the oven to completely dry out.

If you forage (or buy) fresh chestnuts you will (eventually) be rewarded with a sweet, mealy, nutty nub of deliciousness. However there is a very real possibility that along the way you will have given up the will to live, particularly if it is a successful forage and you have a large pile of shiny brown nuts. There is no way we can sugar coat this (if you want to sugar coat chestnuts you need to peel them first): peeling chestnuts is frustrating. You need to remove both the hard outside shell and the thin brown membrane covering the nut.

Take the nuts and lie them on the flat side and cut a slit through the shell. Put the nuts into a bowl of water and soak for 5 minutes.

Roast the chestnuts in a 230°C / 450°F / Gas 8 oven for 15 minutes. Take a small sharp knife and prise off the hard shell, mostly this will take the membrane with it. If it doesn't, scrape off any membrane. The bad news is you need to do this while the nuts are hot so you will need to wear gloves or handle them through a towel to avoid burnt fingers.

Luckily canned and vacuum-packed peeled cooked chestnuts are readily available, but when you are feeling strong do use fresh as they are lovely.

SLICING AND CHOPPING

When slicing nuts it is best to do so when warm as the nuts are softer and less likely to shatter into shards. If you want really thin slivered almonds for presentation it is probably best to buy slivered almonds as you will not be able to get the large thin planes. Very large nuts like Brazil nuts can be shaved using a good vegetable peeler to give thin curls which make a tasty and attractive topping piled on cupcakes or desserts.

GRINDING NUTS

We use a lot of ground nuts in recipes. They make great wheat flour substitutes for those needing a gluten-free diet and provide a welcome texture to cakes and pastry. Ground almonds are readily available but for other varieties you will need to do the grinding yourself. Just toss the nuts into a food processor or blender with a strong blade and pulse 10-15 times until you achieve the desired texture.

Don't be tempted to just turn the processor on and walk away, the pulse switch is your friend. If you over process, the nuts will become oily. If this does happen just dedicate that batch to nut butter and keep right on blending until you get there.

SMOKED NUTS

Home smoked nuts are a revelation and so much nicer than commercial ones. The smoky flavour is subtle and works so well with the sweet meatiness of the nuts. You can add spice or salt depending on your intended end use.

If you are smoking chestnuts, peel them first, hazelnuts should be skinned but almonds can be skin-on or skinned depending on preference.

Soak the nuts in cold water for 10 minutes. Drain. If you are salting or spicing the nuts, toss the drained nuts in the spice mix. Pecans are great tossed in a mixture of cumin, cayenne and sea salt for example and work beautifully in a Cajun salad. Chestnuts tossed with sugar and cinnamon and smoked make an amazing topping chopped and sprinkled over pumpkin pie.

Set up your smoker according to instructions. Spread out the nuts and smoke over wood for 30 minutes. Remove from the smoker and let cool. Eat as a snack or use in salads or in the cabbage gratin on page 127.

Activating Nuts

Nuts and seeds have a protective coating of phytic acid. Phytes are used by the nut or seed as a source of energy in sprouting. Some diet gurus, notably paleo experts, suggest that the phytic acid level should be removed as it can prevent the absorption of certain minerals, particularly calcium, iron and zinc. For this reason they advocate the soaking of nuts prior to use. This is also useful if you are using the nut in a nut cream or blending it, as it softens the nut and reduces the strain on your food processor; but in our view it is unnecessary to soak a nut to activate it and then dehydrate it to make it crispy again. Humankind have been eating nuts basically since we have been eating and our bodies are well set up to regulate the phytic acid levels themselves.

If you decide to activate nuts then you should soak them for around 8 hours (overnight is ideal). You then need to rinse them and if you are not blending, spread them out on trays and either place in a dehydrator or in the oven on its very lowest setting for 8-12 hours.

Nut oils contain many of the healthy nutrients found in nuts, so substituting nut oils in your dressings or as a drizzle over a completed dish is a flavoursome good idea. We particularly advocate using an oil which echoes the flavours of any nuts in a dish. However, as with juicing fruit, extracting oil strips out any of the benefits from fibre (and these are legion).

Also be aware when cooking with nut oil that many have a low burning point compared to sunflower oils and will take on an acrid bitter flavour if they are overheated. The exception is peanut oil (legume, not a nut, darling) which is an excellent cooking medium often used for stir fries.

STORE CUPBOARD STAPLES
OR
SQUIRREL NUTKIN'S LARDER

These are the things you should always squirrel away (sorry couldn't resist) so that your kitchen is well-stocked with nutty staples such as milks, butters and oils which can be used in a wide variety of dishes. A lot of these are now widely available commercially and if time is short do not hesitate to buy a good brand. However if you would like to make your own it is quite simple and here is how.

Nut Butters

Peanut butter used to be the only nut butter you could buy (and delicious it was too) but today a wide variety of nut butters are readily available in the supermarket and health food stores. They are great in baking (use in place of a portion of the butter in biscuit recipes) and make amazingly delicious salad dressings. Match the butter (almond, cashew, hazelnut) to the rest of the dish.

To be honest, the commercial brands are so good we often use them but if you would like to make your own it is simple enough to do, provided you have a powerful blender. If you are planning on a more sophisticated butter, one with the addition of spice or chocolate, it is definitely worth making your own as many commercial varieties have a lot of added sugar, salt or additives. Roasting the nuts before you begin is not essential but will result in a more rounded 'nutty' flavour and is very worthwhile.

To make a 500 g / 1 lb jar

500 g / 1 lb / 4 cups nuts of your choice
2 tablespoons olive oil
pinch of sea salt
honey to taste

Put the nuts into a food processor and pulse till roughly chopped. If you like crunchy nut butter take out a quarter of a cup and reserve. Pulse again until the nuts are ground and the oil in the nuts starts to come out, making the mixture look damp and buttery (this can take about 15 minutes depending on the strength of your food processor). Stop it at intervals and scrape the mix down from the sides of the processor using a spatula. Depending on your nuts you may have to add up to two tablespoons of olive oil. When the required texture is reached, taste and add sea salt and/or honey to suit your own preference and the intended end use. At this point if you are going for crunchy nut butter stir the remaining nuts back in.

Put into a screw top jar and keep in the fridge for up to three weeks. The nut butter will stiffen a bit in the fridge but will soften again at room temperature (or on hot toast!).

Amlou or Moroccon Honey Nut Butter

We first met this on holiday in Morocco where it is a local delicacy made with argan oil. If you can get argan oil this makes it extra special (do make sure you get culinary argan oil and not that intended for cosmetic and hair products!). It is important you let the toasted nuts become completely cold before you grind them or the butter will be greasy. This is traditionally served with flatbreads but is also delicious on waffles or stirred through porridge.

Makes one medium jar

125 g / 4 oz / 1 cup skin-on almonds
4 tablespoons olive or argan oil
sea salt
40 g / 1 ½ oz / 2 tablespoons honey

Preheat the oven to 160°C / 350°F / Gas 3. Spread the almonds in a single layer on a flat baking tray (sheet) and toast in the oven for 15 minutes or until golden brown. Leave until completely cold.

Whizz the nuts in a food processor until finely ground. Add a large pinch of salt and the oil. Stir in the honey. Taste and add more salt if necessary. Put into a jar and store in a cool place.

Chocolate Hazelnut Spread

We are both big fans of Nutella and used to keep a jar in the cupboard for a quick sweet nutty fix. However since we developed our own version this has supplanted the commercial brand. It is just a little bit more grown up (dark chocolate instead of milk) and totally addictive. It makes the ideal filling for our hazelnut kisses (see page 154) or works well on toast or scones for a mid-morning snack.

Makes a small jar

150 g / 5 oz / 1 ¼ cup skinned hazelnuts
1 tablespoon cocoa powder
1 tablespoon icing (confectioners') sugar
50 g / 1 ¾ oz dark (bittersweet) chocolate, finely chopped
60 ml / 2 fl oz / ¼ cup maple syrup
1-2 tablespoons cold water

Preheat the oven to 190°C / 375°F / Gas 5. Put the hazelnuts onto a baking tray (sheet) and toast for 10 minutes or until golden. Allow to cool completely.

Put the nuts, cocoa powder and icing (confectioners') sugar into a powerful blender or Nutribullet and whizz to a fine grind. Add the maple syrup and one tablespoon of water and whizz again. Melt the chocolate in a bain-marie over boiling water (we have always found the best way to do this and prevent the chocolate seizing is to bring a saucepan of water to the boil, turn it off and place the chocolate in a bowl over the water to melt gently in the residual heat and steam). Stir into the nut mixture to make a paste. You may or may not need to add another tablespoon of water to achieve a spreadable consistency.

Keep in the fridge.

Nut Milks

Nut milks are now widely available in supermarkets and health food stores but do read the label carefully as some can contain surprisingly high levels of added sugar, emulsifiers and thickeners. We always go for unsweetened varieties — you can always add extra sugar if your recipe needs it. Alternatively make your own nut milk. This is one case where pre-soaking of the nuts is essential.

To make 500 ml / 1 pint / 2 cups

100 g / 3 ½ oz / 1 cup almonds (or nut of your choice)
pinch of sea salt
½ teaspoon honey (optional)

Soak the almonds in salted water overnight. The next day drain and rinse. Put the drained nuts in a powerful blender or Nutribullet together with 500 ml / 1 pint / 2 cups of water and blend for 2-5 minutes.

Strain the nut milk through cheesecloth, muslin or a clean J-cloth squeezing gently to get all of the liquid out.

Taste and add a little honey or agave nectar if you think it needs it. Discard the leftover pulp. Keep the milk in a closed glass bottle in the fridge for up to three days.

Nut Cream

Although we firmly believe there is nothing better than thick, softly whipped cream (mmm...) as an accompaniment to desserts, if we are entertaining friends with dairy intolerance we often make this nut cream which is deliciously unctuous beside a tart or spooned onto fruit salad.

125 g / 4 oz / 1 cup raw unsalted cashew nuts
1 teaspoon vanilla extract
1 tablespoon maple syrup or honey

Cover the cashews with boiling water and leave to soak for 2-3 hours. Drain and rinse and put into a powerful blender or Nutribullet with the vanilla and maple syrup. Blend until smooth and creamy.

Chill and use as you would whipped cream.

Spiced Nuts

Spiced nuts are fabulous snacking food. Salted nuts are delicious and almost impossible to resist but add in a sprinkle of spice, a little sugar or some citrus and you can match them to any occasion. If you are planning an Indian feast, then flavour your nuts with cumin and turmeric; for tacos and tortillas, then the nuts need chilli and lime. The best thing is you can make them a few days ahead; keep them in an airtight jar and they are all ready to go on the night. We have given here a recipe for Mexican Nuts but tweak it to fit your mood; there are some suggestions at the end. Peanuts are a go-to staple but all sorts of nuts respond well to spicing, match your nut to the cuisine or what is in the cupboard. Cajun pecans, Mexican peanuts or Chinese cashews are all favourites.

Middle Eastern: cumin, tahini, Aleppo pepper
Indian: cumin, garam masala, mustard seeds, turmeric
Cajun: brown sugar, chilli, finely chopped fresh rosemary, salt
Oriental: sesame seeds, ground ginger, Chinese five spice

Mexican Peanuts

125 g / 4 oz / 1 cup raw peanuts
2 ½ tablespoons lime juice
2 tablespoons olive oil
1 tablespoon chipotle powder or paste
2 teaspoons salt
1 teaspoon cayenne pepper

Preheat the oven to 180°C / 350°F / Gas 4. Toss the peanuts with the flavourings. Spread out onto a baking tray (sheet). Bake 15 minutes, take out the tray and give the nuts a good stir. Bake another 15 minutes or until dry and lightly golden. Cool. Store in an airtight jar.

Dukkah

This heavenly spiced nutty dust is a kind of dry dip. Traditionally you serve at the onset of a meal (or as a nibble) with a little bowl of oil and hunks of good bread. You dip the bread into the oil and then into the dukkah and enjoy. However it has a myriad of uses. You can use it as a crust on fish or chicken, dip cooked spears of asparagus in oil, then dukkah or even sprinkle on poached eggs to add an exotic taste of the Middle East to breakfast. Pistachio dukkah is a particularly delectable taste of the casbah.

50 g / 1 ½ oz blanched hazelnuts
8 tablespoons sesame seeds
4 tablespoons coriander seeds
3 tablespoons cumin seeds
1 teaspoon sea salt
freshly ground black pepper

Preheat the oven to 350°C / 180°F / Gas 4.

Spread the hazelnuts and cumin and coriander seeds onto a baking tray (sheet). Bake for 10 minutes or until golden and fragrant. Cool. Whizz in a food processor (or spice grinder) until finely ground, being careful not to over process. You want a fine ground mix not an oily paste.

Toast the sesame seeds in a heavy-bottomed pan until golden. Mix with the nuts and spices and the salt and pepper. Taste and adjust the seasoning level to your preference.

Nut Brittle

Brittles and shards are the latest thing in food decoration. They can be sweet or savoury and add interest and excitement but most of all flavour and a hint of crunch to your finished dish. Consider shards of peanut brittle in a salad or of macadamia poked into the top of a cheesecake. Theoretically, and indeed we have had this work in practice, these will keep for a few days in an airtight tin but it is best to do just a day ahead as the last thing you need preparing for a dinner party is to open a tin of limp brittle.

sunflower oil to grease
100 g / 3 ½ oz / ½ cups caster (superfine) sugar

50 g / 1 ¾ oz / ⅓ cup finely chopped walnut pieces
1 teaspoon caraway seeds
1 teaspoon fennel seeds

Brush oil over a baking tray. Put the sugar in a heavy bottomed pan. Place over medium heat and melt the sugar swirling the pan to make sure it melts evenly. When melted and golden in colour add the walnuts and spices. Stir briefly to ensure the walnuts are evenly distributed through the caramel and carefully pour onto the oiled baking sheet. Leave to cool and harden and then break into shards.

Marzipan

Home-made marzipan is streets ahead of the bought stuff and not difficult to make. You can also make more interesting marzipan – a green one made from pistachios or a rose water scented one for a Middle Eastern cake.

Makes 450 g / 1 lb

225 g / 8 oz / 2 cups ground almonds
125 g / 4 oz / ½ cup golden caster (superfine) sugar
125 g / 4 oz / ½ cup icing (confectioners') sugar
1 egg, beaten
2 teaspoons lemon juice

Mix the sugars and ground almonds in a large bowl. Make a well in the centre and add the beaten egg and lemon juice. Using a knife combine into a dough. Knead briefly until smooth. If it is too wet add a little icing (confectioners') sugar. Do not overwork. Shape into a ball, wrap in cling film (saran wrap) and keep in the fridge until ready to use. If it is in the fridge a while you may have to knead again briefly to make pliable before rolling out.

Sweet Candied Nuts

You can use the same method for any sort of nut for these, but we like skin on almonds.

Makes 2 cups

280 g / 10 oz / 2 cups skin on almonds
1 egg white
100 g / 3 ½ oz / ½ cup white sugar
1 teaspoon ground cinnamon
¼ teaspoon ground ginger
¼ teaspoon ground allspice
¼ teaspoon ground nutmeg
pinch salt

Preheat oven to 300°C / 150°F / Gas 3. Whisk the egg white till frothy. Add the nuts, sugar and spice and toss to combine. Spread out on an oiled baking tray (sheet) and bake for 2 hours until dried and crunchy. Cool.

These will keep up to a month in an airtight screw top jar.

Pickled Walnuts

Pickled walnuts are a particularly British thing (akin to pickled eggs but much nicer). They work brilliantly with cheese or slipped into stews and Delia has an amazing recipe for pork with a pickled walnut stuffing. You start with green walnuts, and we mean literally green while the hard casing is still velvety and soft (June is your moment) and the finished product is a dark, mysterious, almost black condiment. You will need your own walnut trees to make pickled walnuts, as it is almost impossible to buy green walnuts.

Makes 500 g / 1 lb

500 g / 1 lb green or wet walnuts
100 g / 4 oz / ⅜ cup salt
1 teaspoon whole allspice berries
1 teaspoon black peppercorns
a couple of slices of peeled fresh ginger, the size of a pound coin
250 g / 9 oz / 1 cup brown sugar
600 ml / 1 pint malt vinegar

Collect your green walnuts. You want them soft; test by poking a sterilized darning needle into the nut: it should go through completely. Dissolve half the salt in 600 ml / 1 pint of cold water to form a brine. Soak the nuts in the brine for three days. Drain, make up a second batch of brine and soak them for a further week.

Drain well and spread the nuts out in a single layer and leave them to dry out completely. This may take a couple of days. If you have a sunny conservatory, this is the ideal spot. Turn them a few times to ensure they dry completely. At this point the nuts will turn black.

Heat the oven to its lowest setting and place the clean jars into the oven for 10 minutes to ensure they are sterile. Bring the vinegar to the boil with the sugar, allspice and peppercorns and boil for 10 minutes. Pack the walnuts into the jars, place a slice of fresh ginger in each jar and pour over the hot spiced vinegar. Seal and store for one month before using.

NUTS FOR BREAKFAST

Walnut Maple Crumpets with Bacon

This is our new favourite breakfast: a wonderful balance of sweet butter and salty bacon with the added texture of nuts. We could give you a recipe to make your own crumpets, they are not hard but we both know you are going to buy them from the supermarket so let us skip the pretence. This is breakfast and you want to make something impressive and delicious but most of all quick and easy.

You can use ordinary smoked streaky bacon here but if you can get smoked pancetta rashers they are sublime and cook in half the time.

Serves 2

4 crumpets
8 rashers pancetta bacon
50 g / 1½ oz / 3 tablespoons butter
2 tablespoons maple syrup
3 tablespoons finely chopped walnuts

Mash together the maple syrup, nuts and butter. Grill (broil) the crumpets on both sides. Toast the plain side first. Grill the bacon until cooked and lightly crisped on the edges.

Butter the toasted crumpets generously with the walnut butter – butter the holey side, you want the sweet butter to melt down into the crumpet.

Put two crisped rashers of bacon on top. Serve with napkins – this is scrumptiously messy eating.

Chestnut Waffles

This is an ideal Christmas morning breakfast: a sweet/savoury mix with a Yuletide touch provided by the chestnuts. In fact for a truly special Christmas morning serve this with champagne cocktails made with a shot of chestnut liqueur (crème de châtaignes) topped up with champagne (or prosecco if Christmas is already looking a little expensive this year).

We designed this recipe to serve two as indulgent Christmas breakfasts are best à deux. You will need a waffle iron, but it is a perfect excuse to give yourself one as an early Christmas present. Oh, and it is gluten-free if you are worried about that sort of thing.

Tinned or vac-packed chestnuts are fine here; mornings are no time to be faffing about shelling chestnuts. You will only need a couple of chestnuts from the pack but save the rest for use in the stuffing or to toss with the sprouts for Christmas dinner.

Serves 2

60 g / 2 oz / ½ cup chestnut flour
½ teaspoon salt
15 g / ½ oz / 1 tablespoon butter, melted
2 eggs, separated
125 ml / 4 fl oz / ½ cup milk
1 tablespoon chestnuts, finely chopped
3 rashers of bacon
1 marron glacé
15 g / ½ oz / 1 tablespoon butter
maple syrup to drizzle

Whisk together the flour, salt, melted butter, egg yolks and milk to form a smooth batter. Stir in the chopped chestnuts. Beat the egg whites to stiff peaks and fold into the batter.

Heat your waffle iron and grease with a little butter or oil. Remember to turn it over so both sides are heated. If you are cheating and using an electric waffle iron, just plug in and turn on and oil but don't expect to get your Domestic Goddess gold star.

Snip your bacon into strips and grill (broil) or fry until crisp. Keep warm. Chop the marron glacé.

Pour the batter into the iron and cook for two minutes each side over a medium heat or until golden and cooked through. We find this usually makes between 6-8 small quarter-waffles so if you need to repeat, keep the first batch warm in the oven while you cook the second batch.

Turn out onto plates and top each waffle with a knob of butter, shards of crispy bacon, golden nuggets of marron glacé and a drizzle of maple syrup.

Nutty Porridge

This is a warming and sustaining breakfast to take you through the hardest day. You can make a nut porridge which dispenses with the oats entirely, but with Jane's Scottish heritage we wouldn't dare and have stuck to a mix of oats and nuts.

The proportions are the thing here so although we have said half a cup of oats to half a cup of milk and three quarters of a cup of water, for those of a more bird-like appetite make it with one third, one third and a half.

We have just given cup measures here as pre-breakfast is no time to be mucking about weighing things.

Serves 1

½ cup porridge oats
¼ cup chopped walnuts
½ cup almond milk
¾ cup water
¼ cup raisins
maple syrup and yoghurt to serve

Put the oats, nuts, milk and water in a heavy-bottomed saucepan. Bring to the boil, turn down the heat and simmer, stirring constantly until creamy and thick. Remove from the heat, stir in the raisins and top with a spoonful of yoghurt and a drizzle of maple syrup.

Kale Rosti with Mushrooms and Hazelnuts

This makes a fabulous brunch dish. The kale and nuts make it so good for you, you can go straight back to bed afterwards with the newspapers secure in the knowledge you have already ticked the healthy box for the day. You could put a poached egg on top, it would go really well, but Sally doesn't like poached eggs so developed the horseradish cream which complements the crispy kale, earthy mushrooms and sweet nutty hazelnuts.

Serves 2

Sauce
60 ml / 2 fl oz / ¼ cup plain unsweetened yoghurt
2 teaspoons horseradish
squeeze of lemon juice
1 tablespoon olive oil
black pepper

large handful of kale (approximately 45 g / 1 ½ oz)
1 medium potato (approximately 175 g / 6 oz)
1 egg
2 tablespoons plain (all purpose) flour
100 g / 3 ½ oz chestnut mushrooms
1 teaspoon olive oil
knob of butter
45 g / 1 ½ g cobnuts or hazelnuts

Combine all the ingredients for the sauce, taste and adjust the flavouring with a little more lemon juice or a grind more of black pepper to suit your palate.

Bring a pan of water to the boil, add the kale and cook for one minute. Drain and squeeze out as much water as you can.

Peel and grate the potato into a clean tea towel and wring out the starchy water.

Beat the egg to combine and stir in the kale, potato and flour. Stir well.

Slice the mushrooms. Melt the butter and oil together and fry the mushrooms. A few minutes before they are ready toss in the hazelnuts and cook until the mushrooms are soft and the nuts golden.

Heat a heavy-bottomed pan with a thin film of oil. Put tablespoonfuls of the rosti mixture into the pan, press down and fry for about 5 minutes each side until golden and crisp with a meltingly soft centre.

Serve the rosti topped with mushrooms and hazelnuts and a drizzle of the horseradish yoghurt.

NUTS FOR LUNCH AND SUPPER

Carrot and Peanut Soup

This is a store cupboard favourite: rich, warming and cheap to make from things you usually have in the house. If you want to keep this vegetarian, use vegetable stock.

Serves 4

1 onion
5 large carrots
45 g / ½ oz butter / 3 tablespoons butter
½ teaspoon sea salt
750 ml / 1 ¼ pint / 3 cups chicken stock
75 ml / 2 ½ fl oz / ⅓ cup dry sherry
2 tablespoons smooth peanut butter
squeeze of lemon juice
2 tablespoons salted peanuts, chopped

Peel and chop the onion and carrots. Heat the butter in a heavy-bottomed saucepan large enough to hold the finished soup. Sauté for 5 minutes to allow the vegetables to soften but not colour. Add the stock, bring to the boil and simmer for 30 minutes or so until the carrots are soft. Blend until smooth and return to the pan. Stir in the sherry and peanut butter.

Taste and adjust the seasoning to suit your palate with a squeeze of lemon juice, salt and pepper. Warm through and serve garnished with the chopped peanuts.

Brazil Nut and Carrot Loaf

This is Sally's nut roast recipe based on one she used to make as a student. Some ingredients have been upgraded now we no longer have to survive on a meagre student grant – the nuts have become Brazils and the cheese Gruyère (we think it's inherent nuttiness enhances the nuts) but essentially it is the same. We like to serve it with a spiced tomato sauce.

Serves 6

1 tablespoon olive oil
1 onion, finely chopped
125 g / 4 oz / 1 cup fresh brown breadcrumbs
250 g / 8 oz / 2 cup Brazil nuts
3 tablespoons parsley, chopped
2 carrots, grated
2 eggs, beaten
salt and pepper
freshly grated nutmeg
3 tablespoons Gruyère cheese, grated
2 tablespoons sunflower or pumpkin seeds (or a mix)

Sauce
1 onion, finely chopped
1 clove garlic, crushed
400 g / 14 oz can chopped tomatoes
½ teaspoon chilli flakes (chipotle if possible)

1 teaspoon balsamic vinegar
2 tablespoons double (heavy) cream

Oil a 1 litre loaf tin and line with baking paper. Preheat the oven to 180°C / 350°F/ Gas 4.

Heat the oil in a heavy-bottomed pan, add the onion and fry gently over a low heat until softened and translucent but not coloured.

In a large bowl mix breadcrumbs, nuts, onion, parsley, carrots and eggs. Season with salt, pepper and nutmeg. Mix well, we find that hands work best, put into the lined loaf pan and press down firmly. Put the grated cheese on top and sprinkle with the seeds. Put into the oven and bake for 45 minutes until firm and golden.

While the loaf is cooking make the sauce. Soften the onion and garlic in a saucepan, add the tomatoes and chilli and simmer gently for 20 minutes until thickened. Stir in the balsamic and cream and warm through. Season to taste.

Venison and Chestnut Stew with Chestnut Dumplings

This is a real winter warmer, perfect for a cold evening supper lunch after a bracing walk in the country.

Serves 4

500 g / 1 lb diced venison
2 tablespoons plain (all purpose) flour
2 tablespoons oil
2 onions, sliced
100 g / 3 ½ oz mushrooms, quartered
1 clove garlic, chopped
250 ml / 8 fl oz / 1 cup red wine
250 ml / 8 fl oz / 1 cup beef stock
1 bay leaf
1 sprig rosemary
salt and pepper to taste

Dumplings
50 g / 1 ½ oz chestnut flour
50 g / 1 ½ oz suet
pinch baking powder
25 g / ¾ oz cooked chestnuts, finely chopped

Toss the venison cubes in seasoned flour. Heat one tablespoon of oil in a heavy-bottomed casserole dish and fry (sauté) the venison cubes until brown. Do this in batches to avoid overcrowding the pan and stewing the meat. Set the meat aside.

Add the other tablespoon of oil and fry (sauté) the onion until softened (5-10 minutes). Add the mushrooms and fry another few minutes. Add the garlic and fry one more minute until fragrant.

Return the meat to the pan. Add the red wine and let it bubble up for a few minutes. Add enough beef stock to just cover the meat, you may not need it all. Bring to a gentle simmer and put on the lid. Simmer for 2 hours or until the meat is tender. You can do this on the stove top on a very low heat or in the oven at 150°C / 300°F / Gas 2.

Preheat the oven to 180°C / 350°F / Gas 4.

To make the dumplings put all the ingredients into a bowl and rub in the suet with your fingers until the mixture resembles breadcrumbs. Add just enough cold water to bind. Dust your hands with flour and roll tablespoons of the dumpling mixture into small balls.

Dot the dumplings over the surface of the stew and put into the preheated oven for 30 minutes.

Veal T-bones with Brazil Nut Sauce

This makes an impressive main course for a special dinner for two. It's not that it's difficult to make, far from it, but veal T-bone is an expensive cut and it would require a small mortgage to serve this for a dinner party for twelve but for someone you really want to impress, this is the one. Make sure you choose ethically-raised rose veal.

Serves 2

2 veal T-bone steaks approximately 35 mm / 1 ½ inch thick
2 tablespoons oil
salt and pepper
75 g / 2 ½ oz Brazil nuts
1 tablespoon butter
1 banana shallot
1 clove of garlic crushed
60 ml / 2 fl oz / ¼ cup brandy
180 ml / 6 fl oz / ¾ cup beef stock (or veal stock if you can get it)
dash of double (heavy) cream
1 tablespoon finely chopped rosemary

Put the veal steaks in a dish, massage in the oil, season well and leave to rest for 30 minutes. Heat the oven to 180°C / 350°F / Gas 4.

Grind 45 g / 1 ½ oz of the Brazil nuts to the consistency of ground almonds, chop the remainder. We like to cut them lengthwise in slivers but there is no need to be too precious, you just want a little texture.

Melt the butter in a small heavy-bottomed sauté pan. Gently fry the shallots and garlic until soft but not coloured. Add in the chopped rosemary and give it a stir. Pour in the brandy and cook until nearly completely disappeared. Add in the stock and reduce by half.

Heat a heavy ridged pan. Cook the veal steaks 2-3 minutes each side. Do not move them about, as you are aiming for good char lines. If there is a fat collar on the outside of the steaks hold this down against the pan (use tongs) and cook till the fat is translucent and cooked through (or if you are not a fat eater cut it off after you have cooked the steak, it is better to leave it on during cooking to prevent the meat drying out). Put the pan into the oven for 10 minutes.

After 10 minutes remove the pan from the oven and rest the meat while you finish the sauce.

Stir the ground Brazil nuts into the pan residues and bubble up till heated through. Add a splash of cream for richness.

Serve the steaks with the sauce, sprinkled with the chopped nuts and the remainder of the rosemary.

This is delicious with plain steamed baby potatoes and fresh asparagus.

Leek and Cheese Tart with Cobnut Crumble

This is an unusual but delicious autumnal lunch. We've used hazelnuts in the crust because they have an affinity with cobnuts but are slightly drier than fresh cobs, so work better in pastry. This nutty textured tart case is great for all sorts of fillings. You want a fairly deep quiche or tart tin here as the balance between a creamy layer of cheese and leeks and the nutty base and crumble toppings is what makes this work so well; too thin a creamy layer and it can be a bit dry.

Serves 4-6

100 g / 3 ½ oz / 1 cup oats
60 g / 2 oz / ⅓ cup hazelnuts
30 g / 1 oz Parmesan, finely grated
½ teaspoon salt
45 g / 1 ½ oz / 3 tablespoons butter
1 egg
60 g / 2 oz / ¼ cup fresh cobnuts in the shell
1 tablespoon oil
2 leeks
60 g / 2 oz / ½ cup flour
30 g / 1 oz / 2 tablespoons butter
3 eggs plus 1 yolk
125 ml / 4 fl oz / ½ cup double (heavy) cream
150 g / 5 oz Caerphilly cheese (or another sharp white cheese)

Preheat oven to 180°C / 350°F / Gas 4.

Put the oats and hazelnuts onto a tray and toast for 10 minutes until lightly golden. Watch the tray and give it a stir at half time to ensure it browns evenly. Let it cool completely. Whizz in the food processor until you have a coarse-textured flour. As always with nuts don't over process or it will become oily. Add the Parmesan, salt and butter and pulse just till combined. Add the egg and pulse very briefly to form a dough.

This is a delicate crumbly pastry but it is quite forgiving so we find the best way to handle it is to lay a sheet of cling film (saran wrap) slightly larger than your tart tin (use a 20 cm / 8 inch metal tin) on the bench, put the dough onto this and then place another layer of film (wrap) on top. Roll or press out to the size of the tin. Remove the top layer of wrap and lifting the bottom layer place down into the tin, pressing out to fill any spaces. Fill with baking paper and baking beans and bake blind for 15 minutes.

Remove the shells from the cobnuts (we find a firm hand with the meat mallet does the trick) and chop coarsely. Mix with the flour, season and rub in the butter.

Finely slice the white part of the leeks. Heat the oil and fry the leeks gently till softened but not coloured. Beat the eggs and cream. Season, stir through the leeks and crumble in the Caerphilly cheese. Pour into the tart case. Top with the crumble and bake for 30 minutes or until the top is golden and the filling is set.

Serve with a salad of endive (chicory) and lettuce with a sharp dressing.

Almond Crusted Cauliflower with Salsa Verde

We've put this in the main course chapter although really it is more of a starter or light lunch.

Serves 4 as starter or 2 as light lunch

half a small cauliflower, divided into florets
plain (all purpose) flour (enough to coat the cauliflower)
2 eggs, beaten
60 g / 2 oz / ½ cup finely chopped almonds
30 g / 1 oz / ¼ cup cornmeal
½ teaspoon smoked paprika

oil for deep frying

Salsa Verde
good handful of parsley
good handful of mint
1 tablespoon capers
1 tablespoon green olives
3 anchovies, chopped
60 ml / 2 fl oz / ¼ cup olive oil

Put the flour in one bowl and the eggs in another. In the third bowl mix the chopped almonds and cornmeal with the paprika. Dip the florets into the flour then the egg and finally the almond mix.

Make the salsa verde by chopping all the ingredients (except the oil) finely, mixing together stir in the oil to make a chunky sauce. Taste and adjust the balance to taste by adding a little more oil, herbs or capers.

Heat the oil in a deep fryer. Deep fry the cauliflower florets for a few minutes until golden. Drain on kitchen paper and serve with salsa verde.

LOUY'S NUT WELLINGTON

Every Christmas, Jane spends the day with friends who are vegetarians. A die-hard lover of turkey, it was a worry as to how she would cope without a 'traditional' Christmas dinner. One Christmas was all it took for her to be converted; served with all the trimmings (yes, roast potatoes, roast parsnips, bread sauce, cranberry sauce, stuffing, gravy, sprouts and peas for the sprout-haters) this makes an wonderful Christmas meal.

It may look as if there are a lot of ingredients in this recipe but most of them are things that you will probably have in your cupboards anyway. The quantities are easy-going; this is the way we like it but you can add more or less of any of the herbs and spices as you wish.

Serves 8-12, depending on the amount of trimmings you add.

50 g / 2 oz / 3 ½ tablespoons butter
1 onion, chopped
2 cloves garlic
2-4 sticks celery, chopped very finely
2 tablespoons plain (all purpose) flour
pinch dried chilli
1 teaspoon chopped thyme
1 teaspoon chopped sage
1 teaspoon marjoram
1 teaspoon ground cumin
salt and black pepper to taste
150 ml / 5 fl oz / ⅔ cup vegetable stock
150 ml / 5 fl oz / ⅔ cup red wine
350 g / 12 oz / 3 cups ground cashew nuts
225 g / 8 oz chopped chestnuts. The ready-cooked vacuum-packed ones are best.
175 g / 6 oz breadcrumbs. You may need more if the mixture is sloppy.
110 g / 4 oz Gruyère cheese, grated

200 g / 7 oz tin tomatoes, chopped
2 tablespoons fresh parsley, chopped
1 tablespoon Worcestershire sauce
a sheet of puff pastry. This is definitely one of those occasions
when it is worth using ready-made pastry
flour for rolling
cream or milk, to glaze

Heat the oven to 200°C / 400°F / Gas 6

Melt the butter in a frying pan and fry the onion, garlic and celery till lightly browned. Stir in the herbs, spices and flour and allow to cook for a few moments, stirring all the time, until the butter and flour mixture (roux) is well mixed. Add the vegetable stock and wine, whisking all the time. When the sauce has thickened remove from the heat and set aside.

Mix the nuts and breadcrumbs together in a large bowl. Add the onion mixture, grated cheese, tomatoes, parsley and Worcestershire sauce. Mix well. It should be sticky but manageable. If it is very sloppy, add more breadcrumbs otherwise your pastry will get a dreaded soggy bottom.

Grease a large baking sheet. Roll out the pastry as thinly as you can into a rough oblong and transfer onto the baking sheet. Pile the mixture into the centre and bring the sides of the pastry up to form a giant, flattish sausage. Stick the edges firmly together using water as glue. Make air slits and brush with cream or milk.

Bake for 30-40 minutes. If the pastry looks as if it is burning you can turn the oven down a bit or cover the pie with tinfoil.

Savoury Nut Cheesecake

This is a richly decadent savoury main course perfect for a special vegetarian dinner. Like all cheesecakes, it needs to be made ahead, so it is also ideal for a buffet spread. Serve in small slices. It is rich and goes perfectly with a slightly bitter green salad made with endive (chicory).

Serves 10

Base
150 g / 5 oz cream crackers (saltines)
100 g / 3 ½ oz / 1 cup walnuts
125 g / 4 oz / 1 stick unsalted butter

Filling
250 g / 8 oz / 1 cup ricotta cheese
250 g / 8 oz / 1 cup cream cheese
150 g / 5 oz strong blue cheese (Stilton is good)
4 eggs, beaten
mustard cress

Whizz the crackers (saltines) and nuts in the food processor until they are fine crumbs. Melt the butter on the stove or in the microwave and mix into the crumbs. Press the mix over the base and up the sides of a loose-bottomed cake tin. Put into the fridge to rest for 30 minutes.

Preheat the oven to 150°F / 300°F / Gas 2. Beat the cheeses together with the eggs. Season and pour onto the base. Put the tin onto a baking tray (sheet) and put in the oven. Bake for about one hour and 15 minutes or until set (don't worry about a slightly wobbly centre, this will firm up as it cools). Run a knife around the edge of the tin to free the filling from the sides. Turn off the oven, leave the door slightly ajar and let the cheesecake cool. You can leave this overnight.

Keep in the fridge but take out about an hour before you want to eat it. Sprinkle the top with mustard cress and serve with a spicy chutney.

NUTTY SIDE DISHES AND SALADS

BEETROOT WITH PISTACHIOS

This is a great summer salad, colourful and delicious and perfect for a barbecue. It can be served warm or cold. If time is short or you don't want purple fingers, then by all means use pre-cooked vacuum-packed beetroot and bake, drizzled with a little balsamic for 20 minutes to caramelize the edges.

Serves 4-6

4 medium beetroot (beets)
100 ml / 3 ½ fl oz / ½ cup plain unsweetened yoghurt
(preferably Greek)
1 tablespoon lemon juice
50 g / 1 ½ oz pistachios (unsalted and shelled)
salt to taste
2 tablespoons mint leaves, finely sliced

Preheat the oven to 200°C / 400°F / Gas 6. Place the beetroot (beets) on a baking tray (sheet). Bake for 45 minutes to an hour or until tender. Leave till cool enough to peel. Cut into chunky wedges.

Mix the yoghurt with lemon juice and season. Chop the pistachios finely and mix into the yoghurt. Spoon over the beetroot (beets). Sprinkle with chopped mint.

Autumn Slaw

This elegantly white slaw makes the most of autumnal ingredients and the celeriac and apple marry beautifully with cobnuts. If cobnuts are not in season, you can use hazelnuts instead.

Serves 4-6 as side salad

Dressing
2 tablespoons mayonnaise
1 tablespoon plain yoghurt
1 teaspoon Dijon mustard
1 teaspoon maple syrup

squeeze of lemon juice
salt and pepper to taste

½ celeriac
1 tart, crunchy eating apple
½ fennel
½ Savoy cabbage, finely sliced
15 fresh cobnuts

Make the dressing by combining all the ingredients, taste and season. Add a little more lemon juice if you think it needs it.

Peel the celeriac and cut into thin matchsticks. Halve the fennel and slice into thin matchsticks. If you are not going to dress the slaw immediately then you will need to put the celeriac and the fennel into cold water with a squeeze of lemon juice to prevent them discolouring. Peel and core the apple, cut into matchsticks and put into the acidulated water with the celeriac and fennel.

When you are ready to serve, drain the vegetables and put them in a bowl with the sliced cabbage and toss to mix well. Add the dressing and toss again, you want a thin coating of dressing evenly through the salad.

Preheat the oven to 180°C / 350°F / Gas 4. Shell the cobnuts (we find a meat mallet works well) and chop coarsely. Put onto a tray and toast in the oven for 5 minutes until lightly golden and nutty smelling. Set aside to cool.

Just before serving, add the cobnuts and toss a final time to distribute them through the salad.

PUMPKIN WITH CHESTNUTS

A delicious accompaniment to roast poultry, this works well with the turkey at Thanksgiving or Christmas.

Serves 6

1 medium pumpkin or butternut squash
1 tablespoon dark brown sugar
1 tablespoon olive oil or melted butter
½ teaspoon cinnamon
75 g / 2 ½ oz / ½ cup cooked vacuum-packed chestnuts

Preheat your oven to 180°C / 350°F / Gas 4. Peel the pumpkin, take out the seeds and cut into large chunks. Toss with oil and put into a baking dish. Sprinkle with brown sugar and cinnamon. Tuck the chestnuts in round the chunks of pumpkin and bake for 30-40 minutes until tender and slightly caramelized.

CABBAGE AND SMOKED CHESTNUT GRATIN

This is divine and one instance when it is worth the pain of peeling fresh chestnuts. It makes a luxurious accompaniment to game or can stand alone as a vegetarian main course.

For instructions on how to smoke chestnuts see page 99. Use plain smoked nuts, not sweetened or spiced.

Serves 6-8 as a side dish, 4 as main course

1 tablespoon butter
350 g / 12 oz white or Savoy cabbage
250 ml / 8 fl oz / 1 cup crème fraîche
100 g / 3 ½ oz Comté cheese
60 g / 2 oz / ½ cup smoked chestnuts, coarsely chopped
black pepper
a little ground fresh nutmeg
3 tablespoons fresh breadcrumbs

Preheat the oven to 200°C / 400°F / Gas 6. Butter a gratin dish using half the butter.

Bring a pot of salted water to the boil and blanch the cabbage leaves for 5 minutes. Drain well and pat dry with kitchen towel. Roll the leaves and chop finely across the grain to give fine ribbons.

Put one third of the cabbage in the bottom of the gratin dish, sprinkle with a third of the chestnuts and a third of the cheese. Spoon over a third of the crème fraîche. Season well with black pepper and nutmeg. Repeat twice more to use up the ingredients. Sprinkle the breadcrumbs over the top and dot with remaining butter.

Bake for 30 minutes until the top is golden and the gratin bubbling round the edges.

Lettuce, Blue Cheese and Walnut Salad

A lovely simple salad that takes minutes to make and goes with everything. For a more substantial lunch salad, add crispy bacon lardons and crunchy croutons (if you can get walnut bread, use this for the croutons, but make sure it is just walnut bread, not walnut and raisin, that would be weird). If you can get cucomelons those little cucumber/melon crosses that are available now in summer, they are wonderfully fresh and crunchy here.

Serves 4-6 as a side salad

1 head of cos (romaine) lettuce
50 g / 1 ½ oz toasted walnuts
half a medium cucumber, seeded and sliced
blue cheese (something soft and tangy like Gorgonzola or Bleu d'Alembert)

Vinaigrette
2 tablespoons walnut oil
1 tablespoon olive oil
1 tablespoon sherry vinegar
salt and pepper to taste

Wash the lettuce and pat dry. Tear into bite-sized pieces and put into a salad bowl. Add the toasted walnuts and cucumber (or cucomelon).

Put all of the vinaigrette ingredients into a screw-top jar. Do up tight and shake vigorously to emulsify. Taste and adjust the seasoning if necessary. Add to the salad, toss well and crumble over the blue cheese.

Cajun Pumpkin Salad

This is a tasty and colourful barbecue salad substantial enough to serve for lunch. If you are feeling lazy or in a rush, you could use a small can of sweet corn instead of the blackened corn, but if you can do use fresh corn as it does make a difference. If you are cooking for vegetarians just leave the bacon out.

100 g / 3 ½ oz / 1 cup pecan nuts
2 tablespoons honey
½ teaspoon sea salt
1 tablespoon golden caster (superfine) sugar
¼ teaspoon cayenne pepper
1 cob of sweet corn
2 rashers streaky bacon
1 medium pumpkin or butternut squash
1 tablespoon soft brown sugar
½ teaspoon of smoked paprika
100 g / 3 ½ oz green beans
100 g / 3 ½ oz cherry tomatoes
handful of rocket

Dressing
1 teaspoon Dijon mustard
1 clove garlic, crushed
1 tablespoon tomato ketchup
1 teaspoon Cajun spices
¼ cup olive oil
1 tablespoon red wine vinegar
salt and pepper

To caramelize the nuts, preheat the oven to 200°C / 400°F / Gas 6. Put the nuts, honey, salt and the first measure of sugar and cayenne in a small bowl and stir well making sure the nuts are evenly coated. Spread out on a non-stick baking tray (sheet) and bake for 5 minutes. Take out and leave to cool.

Heat a ridged griddle pan over a high heat. Strip the husk and silk from the corn cob, oil lightly and cook until lightly toasted on all sides; if a few kernels blacken don't panic as this just adds to the charm. Using a sharp knife, strip the kernels and reserve, and discard the cob.

Griddle the bacon until cooked and crispy and snip into small pieces.

Peel the pumpkin and chop into 1 inch cubes. Put onto a lightly oiled baking tray (sheet) and sprinkle with brown sugar and cayenne. Bake for 30 minutes until the pumpkin is soft but still holding its shape. Cool.

Blanch the green beans.

To make the dressing whisk all the ingredients together until emulsified.

Toss together the cubed pumpkin, corn, bacon, beans, cherry tomatoes and rocket. Toss with dressing.

Nutty Couscous

This is the ideal accompaniment for a tagine. Any leftovers make an easy and delicious packed lunch, just add a little crumbled feta cheese. Barberries are readily available from Middle Eastern shops or online but if you have trouble finding them you can use cranberries.

Serves 4 as a side dish

25 g / 1 oz / 2 tablespoons butter
200g / 7 oz / 1 cup couscous
salt and pepper
1 tablespoon olive oil

30 g / 1 oz barberries
25 g / 1 oz chopped almonds
25 g / 1 oz chopped pistachios
15 g / ½ oz pine nuts
1 tablespoon finely shredded mint
2 tablespoons finely chopped coriander

Preheat the oven to 120°C / 250°F / Gas Slow. Melt the butter in a heavy-bottomed pan (skillet) which you can put in the oven. Add the couscous and cook for about 5 minutes until lightly golden. Add in 400 ml / 13 ⅔ fl oz / 1 ½ cups of recently boiled water. Stir well, cover the pan (skillet) with foil and put in the oven for 10 minutes.

Take the couscous out of the oven, remove the foil, season well, add the olive oil and fluff it up with a fork. Stir through the barberries, nuts and herbs. Serve.

SAUCES AND DRESSINGS

Tarator

Tarator is a Turkish dish half way between a sauce and a dip. Made with breadcrumbs and walnuts, herbs, oil and vinegar, it is delicious on green beans or peppers or works well with fish. Here we have played fast and loose with tradition, as is our wont, and made it with Brazil nuts. This makes it slightly more luxurious and removes the slightly greyish-purplish hue that sometimes happens with ground walnuts.

Don't even think of making this with pappy commercial white bread. You need a firm-textured white loaf, but not brown as this gives the sauce a very unappetising colour.

2 slices good white bread
75 g / 2 ½ oz / ¼ cup Brazil nuts
2 cloves garlic
75 ml / 2 ½ fl oz / ⅓ cup olive oil

30 ml / 1 fl oz / 2 tablespoons sherry vinegar
salt, pepper and sweet smoked paprika

Cut the crusts from the bread. Chop the nuts and crush the garlic with a little salt. Moisten the bread with cold water and then squeeze it out with your hands leaving a white, bread dough. Put into a food processor, add the oil gradually until absorbed, then the nuts and garlic. Finally add in the vinegar. It should have a smooth creamy consistency similar to mayonnaise. Taste, season and add a little more oil or vinegar if required or if the balance is just right you can thin with a little water. Serve sprinkled with smoked paprika.

PICADA

This Spanish nutty breadcrumb mix is used to thicken and flavour stews and sauces. Add it just at the last minute so the herbs keep their freshness and the nuts their crunch. Traditionally this is made in a mortar and pestle and you can do this if you wish, but a blender or food processor is much quicker and easier.

a slice of coarse textured good bread
drizzle olive oil
2 cloves of garlic, crushed with a pinch of sea salt
30 g / 1 oz / ¼ cup blanched almonds
2 tablespoons parsley
2 tablespoons olive oil

Preheat the oven to 180°C / 350°F / Gas 4. Tear the bread into large chunks. Put the bread onto a baking tray (baking sheet). Sprinkle with olive oil and salt, and bake for 15 minutes until golden and crisp. Cool.

Put the bread, almonds, garlic and parsley into a food processor and whizz to make crumbs. Leave a little texture. Stir in the oil to form a paste. Taste and season if required.

Australian chef Ross Dobson makes the best satay we have ever tasted. Once you have made this you will never look back. The recipe sounds weird (it includes condensed milk) but trust us, it is amazing.

Serves 4 as part of a barbecue or 2 as a main course

Marinade
4 spring onions (scallions)
80 g / 2 oz / ½ cup peanuts, chopped
2 tablespoons curry powder
125 ml / 4 fl oz / ½ cup condensed milk
125 ml / 4 fl oz / ½ cup coconut cream
2 tablespoons fish sauce
½ teaspoon turmeric
2 tablespoons brown sugar

400 g / 14 oz rump steak
2 tablespoons salted peanuts, crushed

Chop the white part of the spring onions (scallions) and whizz in a food processor with the other marinade ingredients until you have a runny mixture with a little bit of texture from the crushed peanuts. Cut the beef into long thin strips and put in a dish and cover with the marinade; massage in the marinade and leave to rest in the fridge for three hours or overnight.

Remove the meat from the marinade, thread onto metal skewers and cook on a barbecue or under the grill 3-4 minutes each side or until cooked to your liking (we like ours slightly pink). Remove and sprinkle with the reserved peanuts and serve with some sweet chilli sauce.

Herb and Walnut Sauce

This works as a dip or salad dressing and makes a beautiful sauce for fish.

> *clove of garlic*
> *sea salt*
> *250 ml / 8 fl oz / 1 cup plain unsweetened yoghurt*
> *60 g / 2 oz / ½ cup chopped walnuts*
> *60 ml / 2 fl oz / ¼ cup walnut oil*
> *60 ml / 2 fl oz / ¼ cup olive oil*
> *2 tablespoons chopped parsley*
> *1 tablespoon chopped dill*
> *1 tablespoon chopped basil*
> *1 tablespoon lemon juice*

Crush the garlic with a good pinch of sea salt. Add to the yoghurt and stir in the rest of the ingredients.

Pesto

The classic pesto is from Genoa and is a mix of pine nuts, basil and Parmesan. However any herby, nutty paste can be considered a pesto.

Try walnut/parsley or coriander/chilli/peanut. Match your pesto to the dish or serve with crackers or the Parmesan Walnut Shortbreads (see page 153) or toss through boiled new potatoes or pasta.

Cashew Nut Pesto

2 cloves of garlic
pinch of sea salt
100 g / 3 ½ oz / 1 cup cashew nuts
bunch of basil
60 g / 2 oz Parmesan cheese, finely grated
150 ml / 5 fl oz / 2/3 cup olive oil

Crush the garlic with the salt to give a thick creamy paste. Grind the nuts in a processor (or mortar and pestle if you want to tune in to your inner peasant). Add the basil and pulse or pound to thick green slurry. Stir in the cheese and gradually trickle in the oil stirring continuously to give a thick emulsion.

Hazelnut Balsamic Drizzle

On holiday in Devon, we discovered an absolutely delicious hazelnut balsamic drizzle at Powderham Castle farm shop. The perfect balance of sweet, tart and nutty, it was great drizzled over salads or oven-roast vegetables. Sadly it was so good we soon ran out ('I told you we should have bought the larger bottle') and 200 miles is a long way to drive for salad dressing. This is our approximation.

Makes ½ cup:

60 g / 2 oz / ½ cup hazelnuts
125 ml / 4 fl oz / ½ cup good balsamic vinegar
1 tablespoon hazelnut oil
1 teaspoon date syrup

Put the nuts onto a baking tray (sheet) and toast for 10 minutes until golden. Put the nuts in a food processor and grind to a fine grain. This is one case where you can't really over process as a little oil won't hurt.

Whisk together the oil and vinegar, whisk in the date syrup and nuts. Continue whisking until you have a smooth thick drizzle. Taste and season if necessary.

DESSERTS AND PUDDINGS

Christmas Meringue Wreath

If you really want to go all out on Christmas decoration bling you can decorate this with gold leaf but it is really delicious as is. You can make the meringues the day before, or even a couple of days ahead and keep in an airtight tin.

As always, we have based our meringue method on Yotam Ottolenghi's. This was a revelation to us in meringue making and we have never looked back. You can pipe two rings and sandwich them with filling if you prefer, but we find this tends to crack when cutting to serve so we usually make a series of smaller meringue 'buns' and stick them together with the cream to make a wreath shape. You can then just pull it apart to serve each person one or two smaller meringues.

A word on maraschino cherries. Do not even contemplate the 1950s cocktail cherries. There are absolutely excellent luxury maraschinos available now (our favourite is the Croatian brand Luxardo) and this is what you want. If you can't get these, then good quality fresh or frozen dark cherries are a perfectly acceptable substitute.

300 g / 10 oz / 1 ¼ cup caster (superfine) sugar
4 large egg whites
pinch salt
300 ml / 10 fl oz / 1 ¼ cup double (heavy) cream
3 marrons glacés, chopped
3 tablespoons maraschino cherries, drained

100 g / 3 ½ oz dark (bittersweet) chocolate
2 tablespoons chestnut liqueur to drizzle
gold leaf to decorate

Preheat the oven to 200°C / 400°F / Gas 6. Line a baking tray with baking paper and mark out 12 circles the size you would like your meringues (we find drawing round a glass or teacup about right).

Spread the sugar over an oven tray (baking sheet) lined with baking paper. Place in the oven for about 8-10 minutes until the sugar is hot and just beginning to melt a little around the edges. Turn the oven down to 110°C / 250°F / Gas ½.

Beat the egg whites and salt till just beginning to stiffen. Add the hot sugar gradually while constantly whisking and keep whisking until the mixture has cooled and is thick and glossy, around 10 minutes. Pipe or spoon (depending on how sophisticated you want to be) the meringue mixture onto the circles. Put in the oven and bake for about 2 hours or until dry. Turn off the oven and leave the meringues in there with the door ajar to cool completely.

The meringues can be stored in an airtight tin for several days but don't fill them until you are ready to serve.

Whip the cream to soft peaks. Stir through the marron glacé and cherries and use to fill and stick together the meringues in a wreath shape.

Melt the chocolate in a bain-marie and drizzle it and the chestnut liqueur over the wreath to serve. Decorate with gold leaf if using.

Mont Blanc Tartlets

Another perfect alternative to Christmas pudding. I know we do seem to go chestnutastic at Christmas but really there is something quintessentially Christmassy about chestnuts. They add a glorious Dickensian flavour to the festivities. You can of course serve these anytime as a dinner party dessert and in fact we whipped up a batch for the Wine Club's sweet wine and port tasting where the unctuous nutty sweetness went perfectly with the rich sweet Amarone.

The recipe makes little tartlets for a sweet treat after a big meal but do make them slightly larger if you like, just remember to make the meringue 'hats' the same diameter as your tart cases.

Makes 12 5 cm / 2 inch tartlets

Meringues
150 g / 5 oz / 1 ¼ cup caster (superfine) sugar
2 large egg whites
pinch salt

Pastry
150 g / 5 oz / 1 ¼ cup plain (all purpose) flour
30 g / 1 oz / ¼ cup ground almonds
90 g / 3 oz / ¾ stick unsalted butter
1 tablespoon icing (confectioners') sugar
1 egg yolk
iced water if necessary

Filling
400 g / 14 oz tin chestnut purée
250 ml / 8 fl oz / 1 cup double (heavy cream)
1 tablespoon icing (confectioners') sugar, omit if the chestnut
puree is already sweetened
1 tablespoon dark rum
3 marrons glacés, chopped

You can make the meringues the day before, or even a couple of days ahead and keep in an airtight tin. In fact, we would recommend this as meringues take a while to cook and unless you have a double oven you can't cook them at the same time as the pastry cases.

Preheat the oven to 200°C / 400°F / Gas 6. Line a baking tray with baking paper and mark out 12 circles the diameter of your tart tins.

Spread the sugar over an oven tray (baking sheet) lined with baking paper. Place in the oven for about 8-10 minutes until the sugar is hot and just beginning to melt a little around the edges. Turn the oven down to 110°C / 250°F / Gas ½.

Beat the egg whites till they are just beginning to stiffen. Add the hot sugar gradually while constantly whisking and keep whisking until the mixture has cooled and is thick and glossy, around 10 minutes. Pipe or spoon the meringue mixture onto the circles. Put in the oven and bake for about 2 hours or until dry. Turn off the oven and leave the meringues in there with the door ajar to cool completely.

Preheat the oven to 180°C / 350°F / Gas 4. Make the pastry by pulsing the flour, icing (confectioners') sugar, ground almonds and salt for a few seconds to combine, add butter pulse again to make a texture like breadcrumbs, add the egg yolk, one more pulse to combine to a dough. If too dry add a little iced water. Wrap in plastic wrap (saran wrap) and rest in the fridge for 30 minutes.

Roll out and line the tartlet tins. Fill with baking paper and baking beans and bake blind for 15 minutes. Remove the paper and beans and cook another 10 to 15 minutes until golden, dry and cooked through. Remove from the oven and cool.

No more than an hour before serving whip the cream to soft peaks. Beat the chestnut purée and rum to soften and add the sugar if using. Fold the cream into the chestnut purée with the marron glacé. Fill the tartlet shells and top each tart with a little meringue hat.

White Chocolate and Hazelnut Croissant Butter Pudding

Sally developed this one when she was running her café and sometimes had leftover croissants. It is so good that now, when let's be honest there are never any leftover croissants, she sometimes hides a few just so she can made this delicious pudding.

You can skip the caramelization step if you like but the slightly bitter crunchy topping contrasting with the soft creamy pudding is well worth the 5 minutes it takes to do.

Serves 6

500 ml / 16 fl oz / 2 cups milk
500 ml / 16 fl oz / 2 cups double (heavy) cream
1 vanilla pod
3 eggs
4 egg yolks
200 g / 7 oz / 1 cup golden caster (superfine) sugar
175 g / 6 oz white chocolate, chopped
3 tablespoons Amaretto
4 slightly stale croissants
25 g / 1 oz sultanas
25 g / 1 oz blanched hazelnuts, coarsely chopped
2 tablespoons golden caster (superfine) sugar

Preheat the oven to 200°C / 400°F / Gas 6.

Put the milk and cream into a heavy-bottomed saucepan. Split the vanilla pod and scrape the seeds into the pan. Add the pod itself. Bring to a gentle boil.

Beat the sugar with the whole eggs and the egg yolks until pale and thick. Take the milk off the heat and pour over the egg mixture and stir well. Stir in the chopped chocolate. Add the Amaretto to the custard. Remove the vanilla pod.

Slice the croissants into thick slices and layer, slightly overlapping in a shallow dish. Sprinkle with sultanas and hazelnuts. Pour over the custard. Cover with foil and bake for 15-20 minutes until set.

Remove from the oven and rest for 10 minutes. Sprinkle over the caster (superfine) sugar and caramelize with a blow torch or under a hot grill.

ICED CHESTNUT PARFAIT

Serves 6-8

4 egg yolks

125 g / 4 oz / ½ cup golden caster (superfine) sugar
250 g / 8 oz chestnut purée
50 g / 2 oz / ¼ cup light muscovado sugar
2 tablespoons chestnut liqueur
250 ml / 8 fl oz / 1 cup double (heavy) cream
50 g / 2 oz raisins

Oil a 1 litre loaf or terrine dish and line with cling film (saran wrap).

Beat the egg yolks till pale and thick. Put the sugar into a heavy-bottomed pan with 4 tablespoons of water and dissolve over a low heat. When the sugar is completely dissolved, increase the heat and boil for around 5 minutes until it is just starting to turn golden. Pour onto the egg yolks whisking constantly. Cool.

Beat the chestnut purée with the muscovado sugar and liqueur. Fold into the egg mixture. Whisk the cream to soft peaks and fold into the mixture. Stir in the raisins. Pour into the lined tin and freeze overnight until solid.

Serve in thick slices drizzled with chestnut liqueur.

Peanut Caramel Knickerbocker Glory

Ice cream for grown-ups; this sweet salty mix really works well. This is prettiest if layered up in retro sundae glasses but still tastes delicious if mushed together in a bowl and eaten in your jammies curled up on the sofa in front of a rom-com movie. You can make your own ice cream or use good quality shop bought.

Serves 6

60 g / 2 oz / ½ stick butter
60 g / 2 oz / ¼ cup soft brown sugar
100 ml / 3 ½ fl oz / ⅓ cup double (heavy) cream
30 g / 1 oz dark (bittersweet) chocolate
6 scoops vanilla ice cream
6 scoops hazelnut ice cream

6 scoops chocolate ice cream
8 tablespoons salted peanuts finely chopped

Melt the butter with the brown sugar, stirring constantly. Simmer for five minutes until thick and well combined. Add the cream, stir well, simmer for a couple of minutes and remove from the heat. Cool slightly. You want this to cool a little so it doesn't reduce the ice cream to a puddle but not so much it becomes stiff.

Bring a pan of water to the boil. Put the chocolate into a bain-marie or heatproof bowl. Turn off the heat and place the chocolate over the boiling water to melt. Stir well.

Put a scoop of vanilla ice cream in each sundae glass, drizzle with caramel sauce and add a sprinkle of chopped peanuts. Top with a scoop of hazelnut ice cream, repeat drizzle and sprinkle. Add a scoop of chocolate ice cream and another drizzle of sauce. Take a tablespoon of melted chocolate and drizzle over the top. Finish with a sprinkle of chopped peanuts.

Eat with a long spoon.

CRUMBLE TOPPED PEARS

A single pear half sitting in a pool of caramel custard makes a more sophisticated presentation than a dish of crumble but is just as easy to make. The caramel custard is from Jason Atherton's *Maze* cookbook. It is absolutely delicious and works well with ordinary crumble too.

Serves 6

Caramel custard
165 g / 5 ½ oz / ¾ cup caster (superfine) sugar
150 ml / 5 fl oz / ⅔ cup double (heavy) cream
375 ml / 13 fl oz / 1 ⅔ cup milk
30 g / 1 oz cornflour (cornstarch)
4 egg yolks

3 large dessert pears
100 g / 3 ½ oz / ¾ cup plain (all purpose) flour
60 g / 2 oz / ⅓ cup golden caster (superfine) sugar
60 g / 2 oz / 4 tablespoons cold butter, cubed
60 g / 2 oz / ½ cup hazelnuts

First make the custard. Heat a heavy-bottomed pan over a medium heat. Gradually add the 100 g / 3 ½ oz of the sugar, making sure the sugar melts as it hits the pan. As the sugar melts and caramelizes, swirl the pan to combine. When all the sugar has melted and turned a deep golden brown colour, add 100 ml / 3 ½ fl oz of the cream (be careful as it can spit and molten sugar burns). Swirl to combine and remove from the heat. Cool.

Put the milk into the pan, bring up to the boil. Mix the remaining sugar and the cornflour (cornstarch) in a bowl. Add the egg yolks and beat to a smooth paste. Gradually stir in the last of the cream.

When the milk has come to boiling point, take it off the heat and pour onto the egg yolk mixture stirring continuously. Return to a low heat and, stirring continuously, bring to the boil. Cook for 5 minutes.

Sieve the custard into a clean bowl; cover the surface with cling film (saran wrap) and leave to cool. Once cooled, add the caramel and beat until smooth.

Put the flour, sugar and butter in a food processor and pulse briefly to make a breadcrumb-like texture. Stir in the chopped hazelnuts.

Preheat the oven to 200°C / 400°F / Gas 6.

Peel and halve the pears. Core them, place cut side up in a shallow baking dish and cover the indent and the surface of the pear with crumble. Bake for 25 minutes until golden.

Serve with caramel custard.

Baked Apples

Baked apples are a tremendously comforting nursery pudding, ideal for those autumn or winter nights when you fancy something sweet but don't want to make an effort. The key is to use eating apples not cooking apples which break down and go fluffy. We have two filling options here, a slightly more luxurious one with nuggets of marzipan and a purer more classic one with walnuts and raisins.

Serves 2 (but so easy to scale up)

2 eating apples
1 tablespoon soft brown sugar
½ teaspoon cinnamon
4 walnuts, chopped
2 tablespoons raisins
knob of butter

Preheat the oven to 180°C / 350°F / Gas 4. Core the apples making sure the central cavity is large enough to take the filling. Mix the sugar, cinnamon, nuts and raisins together and lightly pack into the cavity. Put a knob of butter on top of each apple and place in a dish with a splash of water. Bake for 30 minutes until soft. Serve with pouring cream.

Variation: make the stuffing by mixing 2 tablespoons of cranberries with 1 tablespoon of chopped marzipan and 1 tablespoon of chopped almonds.

CASSATA ICE CREAM BOMBE

Traditionally, Sicilian cassata was a sponge cake filled with ricotta, dried fruits and chocolate, encased in marzipan. However, today it is more usually the name given to a layered ice cream dessert. Sally's mother, egged on by her brother, used to make a cassata ice cream dessert every Christmas and this is the recipe we are going to share here. The recipe is not strictly correct, but a family favourite like all our best recipes. You can make all your own ice cream if you are in full domestic goddess mode or buy good quality for the shell of the bombe and just make the centre. You won't need all of the ice cream but extra ice cream in the freezer is never a hardship (or indeed a long term problem).

50 g / 1 ½ oz / ¼ cup raisins
1 tablespoon Amaretto

900 ml / 1 ½ pints vanilla ice cream
475 ml / 1 pint pistachio ice cream
475 ml / 1 pint hazelnut ice cream
75 g / 3 oz / ⅓ cup caster (superfine) sugar
250 ml / 8 fl oz / 1 cup milk
250 g / 8 oz / 1 cup ricotta
40 g / 1 ½ oz / ¼ cup Italian candied lemon peel
30 g / / 1 oz ¼ cup dark (bittersweet) chocolate, chopped
100 g / 3 ½ oz dark (bittersweet) chocolate
1 tablespoon double (heavy) cream

Take the raisins, cover with Amaretto liqueur and leave to soak while you get on with the rest of the bombe.

Take a 1½ litre / 2 ¾ pint plastic or metal bowl (one which can go in the freezer) and line with cling film (saran wrap). Take the vanilla ice cream and let it soften slightly. Spread a thick layer of ice cream over the surface of the bowl and return to the freezer till frozen firm. Take the pistachio ice cream, let soften slightly and spread a thick layer over the vanilla ice cream. Repeat with the hazelnut ice cream.

Beat the sugar into the milk until dissolved, add the ricotta. Churn in an ice cream maker until set. Mix the raisins, mixed peel and chocolate chips and stir into the ice cream mix at the last minute. Use this mixture to fill the centre of the dessert. Put back in the freezer and freeze till firm.

Melt the chocolate and cream in a bain-marie over boiling water. Let cool slightly. Stir well to make a glaze.

Take the ice cream out of the freezer; remove from the bowl, and remove the plastic wrap. Pour the glaze over and serve, or return to the freezer. Remove from the freezer 10 minutes before you want to serve.

Pecan Pie

When catering, we have often been called on to cook pecan pies for American clients celebrating Thanksgiving. As a result we have done a lot of practical research on discovering the very best version (it's a tough job but someone had to do it). Our personal favourite, not entirely traditional but sublimely delicious, is this pecan chocolate version taken from Paul Hollywood's book *How to Bake*.

Serves 10-12

175 g / 6 oz / 1 ½ cups plain (all purpose) flour
30 g / 1 oz pecan nuts
1 tablespoon icing (confectioners') sugar
125 g / 4 oz / 1 stick butter
1 egg yolk
cold water
75 g / 2 ½ oz dark (bittersweet) chocolate
45 g / 1 ½ oz / 3 tablespoons butter
150 g / 5 oz / ⅔ cup golden caster (superfine) sugar
235 ml / 7 ½ ml / ¾ cup golden (corn) syrup
3 eggs
1 teaspoon vanilla extract
225 g / 7 ½ oz / 1 ¾ cup pecan nuts

Preheat the oven to 180°C / 350°F / Gas 4. Place a baking tray (sheet) in the oven.

Finely grind the pecans in a food processor or spice grinder. Add the flour and icing (confectioners') sugar to the food processor. Cut in the butter and whizz briefly to make fine crumbs. Add the egg yolk and pulse briefly to combine. Add just enough water to make a dough.

Rest in the fridge for 30 minutes. Roll out and use to line a 25 cm / 10 inch loose-bottomed pie tin. Line the pie crust with paper and fill with baking beans. Blind bake for 15 minutes.

Bring a saucepan of water to the boil. Remove from the heat. Put the chocolate and butter in a heatproof bowl or bain-marie and place over the hot water and leave to melt, stirring occasionally.

In a medium saucepan combine the sugar and golden (corn) syrup. Bring to the boil, stirring constantly. Cool slightly.

Beat the eggs in a large bowl till frothy. Add the melted chocolate and butter and stir till smoothly combined. Gradually pour in the sugar and golden syrup mixture whisking constantly. Add vanilla extract and stir in the pecans. Set aside to cool completely.

Pour into the blind-baked case and bake for 40 minutes or until the filling is set.

Let cool before serving with thick cold cream.

Almond and Pear Tart

This is a very pretty tart. The pears rise gently above the almond mixture, just waiting for a dollop of cream.

Serves 4 to 6

Pastry
180 g / 6 oz / 1 ⅓ cups plain (all purpose) flour
90 g / 3 oz / 6 tablespoons cold butter, cut into small chunks
water, to bind

Filling
100 g / 3 ½ oz / 7 tablespoons butter, softened
100 g / 3 ½ oz / ½ cup caster (superfine) sugar
½ teaspoon almond extract
2 eggs, lightly beaten
30 g / 1 ¼ oz / 2 tablespoons plain (all purpose) flour
100 g / 3 ½ oz / ¾ cup ground almonds
3 or 4 pears, just ripe, 'Conference' are good.
1 tablespoon lemon juice
2 teaspoons apple jelly

Put the flour into a food processor and blitz briefly so there are no lumps. Add the butter and blitz until the butter and flour are combined and resemble fine breadcrumbs. With the machine running, add cold water a spoonful at a time until the mixture forms a dough. Be careful not to add too much water. Wrap the dough in clingfilm (saran wrap) and put in the fridge for 30 minutes.

Grease a 23 cm / 9 inch tart tin. On a lightly floured surface, roll out the pastry so it lines the base and sides of the tin. Tidy the edges and prick the base with a fork. Return to the fridge for another ½ hour.

Preheat the oven to 200°C / 400°F / Gas 6.

Line the pastry case with greaseproof paper and fill with baking beans. Bake for 15 minutes, remove the beans and paper, reduce the temperature to 180°C / 350°F / Gas 4 and bake for another 5-10 minutes to dry the pastry.

Return the oven to 200°C / 400°F / Gas 6.

Beat the butter, sugar and almond extract together in a bowl. Add the eggs, flour and almonds, mix gently and pour into the pastry case. Peel, halve and core the pears, and brush with lemon juice to stop them turning brown. Arrange the pears cut side down on the almond mixture.

Bake for 30 minutes.

Mix the jelly with a little warm water so it will spread easily. Remove the tart from the oven and brush over with the glaze. Return to the oven for about another 10-20 minutes, until the top is golden and a skewer comes out cleanly.

Leave to cool and serve with lots of thick or clotted cream.

BAKING WITH NUTS

Hazelnut Millionaire's Shortbread

Millionaire's is a favourite childhood treat we are unwilling to let go so we have made the recipe just a little bit more grown-up to enable us to indulge at will. Using hazelnuts in the base and ensuring the chocolate topping is made with 70% dark (bittersweet) chocolate really elevates this slice.

75 g / 3 oz / ½ cup blanched hazelnuts
150 g / 5 oz / 1 ¼ sticks butter
150 g / 5 oz / 1 ¼ cups plain (all purpose) flour
60 g / 2 ½ oz cornflour (cornstarch)
60 g / 2 ½ oz / ⅔ cup icing (confectioners') sugar
200 g / 6 oz / 1 ½ sticks butter
1 can condensed milk
200 g / 6 oz / 1 ½ cups caster (superfine) sugar
200 g / 6 oz dark (bittersweet) chocolate
1 tablespoon golden (corn) syrup
15 g / ½ oz / 1 tablespoon butter

Preheat oven to 180°C / 350°F / Gas 4.

Line a 20 x 25 cm / 8 x 10 inch baking tray at least 5 cm / 2 inches deep.

Place the hazelnuts on an oven tray (cookie sheet) and roast for 10 minutes watching carefully to ensure they don't burn. Cool and put in the food processor and chop very finely. You want a little bit of texture so slightly coarser than ground almonds but no big pieces.

Melt the butter. Mix the flour, cornflour (cornstarch), icing (confectioners') sugar and ground hazelnuts in a bowl. Add the melted butter and mix to a soft dough. Press into the lined tray and bake for 20-25 minutes until the dough is cooked and lightly browned around the edge. Cool completely.

Melt the butter in a large heavy-bottomed pan. Add the condensed milk and sugar and simmer over a low heat until it turns a light caramel colour. Watch this carefully and stir frequently to avoid it catching.

Pour the caramel layer over the cooled base, return to the oven and bake 10 minutes. Allow to cool.

Melt the chocolate, golden (corn) syrup and butter over a bain-marie. When completely melted, pour over the caramel layer and leave to set somewhere cool.

Nuts

Cheesy Nutty Scones

We made these as canapés and served them at the launch of *Berries* where they were hugely popular. Our publisher, Catheryn, insisted we include the recipe in our next book (in fact she may have made it a condition of publication) and so here it is. The idea of scones with tapenade comes from Patricia Wells whose beautiful books on French cookery have long been amongst our favourites.

Makes 20 canapé sized or 8 large scones

125 g / 4 oz / 1 cup plain (all purpose flour)
2 teaspoons baking powder
pinch of salt
15 g / ½ oz / 1 tablespoon butter
30 g / 1 oz / ¼ cup chopped hazelnuts
1 tablespoon finely chopped fresh rosemary
125 g / 4 oz / 1 cup grated Gruyère cheese
175 ml / 6 fl oz / ¾ cup milk
1 egg yolk
1 teaspoon milk or water

Tapenade
½ cup pitted black olives
½ cup chopped dried figs

Preheat the oven to 230°C / 450°F / Gas 8.

Line a baking sheet with baking paper (parchment).

In a large bowl combine the flour, baking powder and salt. Rub the butter into the flour to form fine crumbs (you can do this in a food processor but only pulse, do not over process.)

Stir in the rosemary, chopped nuts and two thirds of the cheese. Add the milk gradually cutting with a knife until the mixture forms a dough. You may not need all the milk.

Roll out to about 3 cm / 1 ½ inch thick and cut into scones. Put onto the baking sheet.

Beat the egg yolk and milk in a cup and use to glaze the top of the scones. Sprinkle with the last of the cheese.

Bake for 10 minutes for canapé size or 15 minutes for full size scones. To check if they are done flip one over, the bottom should be golden brown and sound hollow when tapped. Set on a rack to cool.

For the tapenade just whizz the olives and figs in a food processor to make a paste. Spread onto the split scones to serve.

BISCOTTI

Biscotti, the twice-cooked Italian biscuits, are supremely versatile. You can use any kind of nut and vary the flavours at will: Peter Gordon does a delicious version with macadamia nuts and lemon myrtle, but dried apricots are good, as are pistachio nuts. You can even make a savoury version sliced wafer thin and served in shards to accompany salads.

3 eggs
250 g / 8 oz / 1 cup golden caster (superfine) sugar
250 g / 8 oz / 2 cup plain (all purpose) flour
60 g / 2 oz / ½ cup cashew nuts
60 g / 2 oz / ½ cup hazelnuts
100 g / 3 ½ oz / 1 cup desiccated coconut
1 tablespoon Amaretto
60 g / 2 oz / dried figs, chopped
30 g / 1 oz candied lemon peel, chopped

Preheat oven to 180°C / 350°F / Gas 4. Line a baking tray (sheet) with baking paper (parchment).

Beat the eggs until thick and creamy. Sift flour into a bowl. Stir in sugar, nuts, coconut, Amaretto and dried fruit. Stir the eggs into the dry mixture to form a dough. Shape into a log 3 cm / 1 ¼ inch wide.

Put onto a lined baking tray and bake for around 20 minutes, until golden and cooked through. Remove from the oven; turn down to 150°C / 300°F / Gas 2. Cool slightly and cut at an angle into thin slices. Place the slices onto a lined baking tray and bake again until they are firm and just beginning to colour (around 40 minutes). Cool on a wire rack and store in an airtight tin.

PARMESAN WALNUT SHORTBREADS WITH GOAT'S CHEESE AND SUN-BLUSH TOMATO OLIVE PESTO

Makes 30 canapé sized shortbreads

30 g / 1 oz walnuts
30 g / 1 oz / 4 tablespoons plain (all purpose) flour
¼ teaspoon cayenne pepper
45 g / 1 ½ oz / 3 tablespoons butter
60 g / 2 oz finely grated Parmesan cheese

Pesto
8 black olives, pitted and chopped
6 sun-blush tomatoes, finely chopped
15 g / ½ oz parsley, finely chopped.
100 g / 3 ½ oz creamy goat's cheese

Preheat the oven to 180°C / 350°F / Gas 4. Put the walnuts, flour and cayenne in a food processor and whizz until the walnuts are a fine meal and the nuts and flour are well combined.

Dice the butter and add to the flour with the grated Parmesan. Pulse to form a firm dough.

Roll into a long log shape about 1 ½ inches in diameter and rest in the fridge for at least 30 minutes. At this point you can tightly wrap the log in cling film (saran wrap) and keep in the fridge overnight or freeze for up to three months.

When you are ready to cook the biscuits, heat the oven to 180°C / 350°F / Gas 4. Line a baking tray (sheet) with baking paper (parchment). Cut the dough log into discs and place well-spaced on the baking tray. Bake 10 minutes or until golden brown. Cool on rack.

Finely chop the black olives, sun-blush tomatoes and parsley. Combine. Taste and season.

Top the biscuits with goat's cheese and half a teaspoon of the olive and tomato pesto.

Hazelnut Kisses

These are gentle little kisses not crisp cookies, their soft crumbly texture is part of the charm but it does mean they are best eaten within a day or two of making. Keep the biscuits in an airtight tin and spread with chocolate hazelnut paste before serving.

We find whizzing the nuts with the sugar prevents them from going oily.

Makes 16 kisses (32 biscuits)

50 g / 1 ¾ oz skinned hazelnuts
50 g / 1 ¾ oz / ¼ cup golden caster (superfine) sugar
100 g / 3 ½ oz / ¾ cup plain (all purpose) flour
½ teaspoon baking powder
75 g / 2 ½ oz / ⅔ stick butter, chopped
75 g / 2 ½ oz hazelnut butter
hazelnut chocolate spread (see page 102)

Preheat the oven to 190°C / 375°F / Gas 5. Line a baking tray (sheet) with baking paper.

Toast the hazelnuts for 10 minutes or until golden. Allow to cool completely.

Whizz the hazelnuts in a food processor together with the caster (superfine) sugar until the nuts are similar to ground almonds in texture. Add the flour and baking powder and pulse to combine.

Add the chopped butter and hazelnut butter and pulse until the mixture forms a soft dough. Do not overwork.

Put small teaspoons of mixture well-spaced on the tray. Remember they will spread and puff a little, and you are making little sandwiches, so don't make them too big.

Bake for 15 minutes or until golden. Leave to cool and firm on the tray.

When cool, sandwich together using chocolate hazelnut spread.

Hazelnut Torte

This is a classic chocolate torte simply but elegantly decorated with a shiny chocolate glaze and caramelized nuts. Serve in slim slices with whipped cream.

Serves 10

175 g / 6 oz dark (bittersweet) chocolate
175 g / 6 oz / 1 ½ sticks butter
4 eggs
175 g / 6 oz / ¾ cup golden caster (superfine) sugar
30 g / 1 oz / ¼ cup plain (all purpose) flour
60 g / 2 oz / ½ cup chopped toasted hazelnuts

Glaze
175 g / 6 oz dark (bittersweet) chocolate
125 g / 4 oz / 1 stick butter
1 tablespoon honey
60 g / 2 oz / ¼ cup caster (superfine) sugar
12 blanched hazelnuts

Preheat oven to 180°C / 350°F / Gas 4. Grease and line a 23 cm / 9 inch spring form cake tin with baking paper.

Fill a saucepan with water and bring to the boil. Turn off the heat. Break the chocolate into pieces, cube the butter and put both into a heatproof bowl over the hot water. Leave to melt and stir to combine.

Separate the eggs. Beat the yolks with 100 g / 3 ½ oz / ½ cup of the sugar until pale and thick. Stir in the melted chocolate mixture. Fold in the flour and ground hazelnuts.

Beat the egg whites with a pinch of salt until soft peaks form. Gradually add the remaining sugar and beat until stiff peaks. Fold into the chocolate mixture. Pour into the cake tin. Bake for 40-45 minutes or until a cake skewer inserted in the middle of the cake comes out clean. Cool in the tin on a rack. Release from the tin and cool completely.

Melt the chocolate, butter and honey for the glaze in a bain-marie over hot water. Pour a quarter of the mixture into a small bowl and put in the fridge to chill down and thicken.

Turn the torte upside down so the flattest side is uppermost. Using a palate knife spread a layer of the glaze over the top and sides of the cake making it as smooth as possible. Put the cake into the fridge for 10 minutes to set the glaze. Now take the remaining glaze, you want this to be smooth and pourable but not absolutely runny, so if it has thickened too much just rewarm a little over the hot water. Pour the glaze over the part-glazed torte to give a shiny smooth icing. Smooth a little with a palate knife to ensure an even cover but try not to work too much as it will dull the glaze.

Put the sugar in a cold pan. Melt the sugar gently over a medium heat. Cook gently until the sugar turns a golden amber colour. Add the nuts and swirl around till well covered. Tip out onto a sheet of greaseproof paper and leave to set.

Put the caramelized nuts around the edge of the torte.

Afghans

These chocolate biscuits are an institution in New Zealand where they are available in every café. They are actually less nutty than they taste, the secret ingredient being crushed cornflakes but they always have a walnut half on top and so justify their place here.

Makes about 20

50 g / 1 ¾ oz / 2 cups cornflakes
200 g / 7 oz / 1 ¾ sticks butter

100 g / 3 ½ oz / ½ cups golden caster (superfine) sugar
150 g / 5 ½ oz / 1 ¼ cups plain (all purpose) flour
15 g / 1 oz / 2 tablespoons cocoa powder

Icing
125 g / 4 oz / 1 cup icing (confectioners') sugar
15 g / ½ oz / 2 tablespoons cocoa powder
walnut halves to decorate

Preheat the oven to 180°C / 350°F / Gas 5. Grease a baking tray (baking sheet) with butter and line with baking paper. Put the cornflakes into a plastic bag and using a rolling pin, crush them to fine crumbs. Cream the butter and sugar till light and fluffy. Stir in the flour, cornflakes and cocoa powder. Put tablespoons of the mixture onto the tray (this is a stiffish mixture so it may be easier to make balls with your fingers than take tablespoons), well-spaced apart and bake for 15 minutes. Cool on a rack.

Make the icing by mixing sifted icing (confectioners') sugar, cocoa and a little boiling water to make a paste. Spoon onto the top of the Afghans and top each with half a walnut.

BLØTKAKE

The first time we discovered Bløtkake (pronounced 'blurt-kak-ir') was in Tilly Culme-Seymour's delightful book *Island Summers*. It is a Norwegian birthday cake; at least it was the cake Tilly always had and the moment we read about it we knew we wanted it as our birthday cakes too. It is a wonderful concoction of sponge, cream, fruit and marzipan and makes a perfect centrepiece for any tea table, birthday or otherwise. In the book, the cake has to make a fraught journey in a small boat from the mainland bakery to the island, this is not something we would recommend, although one Jane made survived a bike ride to Piccadilly.

Island Summers does not include a recipe for the cake but when Tilly came to sign her books she confirmed that our recipe was pretty near her original.

Ready-made marzipan is fine for this cake but use white, rather than golden for authenticity. You can use any combination of berries, according to your inclination and what is in season.

Serves at least 12; this is very rich and substantial cake.
Cake
300 g / 10 oz / 3 ½ sticks soft butter
300 g / 10 oz / 1 ⅓ cup caster (superfine) sugar
6 eggs
300 g / 10 oz / 2 ½ cups self-raising flour
2 ½ teaspoons baking powder

Filling
300 ml / 10 fl oz / 1 ¼ cups double (heavy) cream
4 drops vanilla extract
3-4 tablespoons apple juice
3-4 tablespoons strawberry jam
100 g / 3 ½ oz / ¾ cup chopped walnuts

Topping
300 g / 10 oz marzipan
200 g / 7 oz strawberries
200 g / 7 oz blueberries
icing (confectioners') sugar, for rolling out and to dust the finished cake

Preheat the oven to 180°C / 350°F / Gas 4. Grease 3 x 23 cm / 9 inch loose-bottomed cake tins and line the bases with baking parchment. Even if you have to cook them in batches, it is much easier to cook three separate cakes rather than trying to cut one into three layers. They also rise better.

Put the butter and sugar into a bowl and cream together until light and fluffy. Beat in the eggs, one at a time, adding a little flour after each egg. Gently fold in the remaining flour. Pour the mixture into the tins and level out. Bake for about 20-25 minutes. The cake will have pulled away from the sides of the tin and a skewer should come out clean.

Remove from the oven and allow to cool for a few moments. Take the cakes out of the tins, remove the paper and leave on a wire rack to cool completely.

Whip the cream and vanilla extract till it forms reasonably stiff peaks.

Once the cakes are totally cooled, put the bottom layer onto the plate you wish to use; the cake will be almost impossible to move once you have decorated it. Drizzle 1-2 tablespoons of apple juice over the bottom layer of cake; this will ensure it is deliciously moist and gooey. Spread with a layer of ½ the jam and then add a layer of about ⅓ of the cream. Sprinkle half the chopped walnuts on top. Put the next layer of cake on top and repeat the apple juice, jam, cream and walnut layers.

Put the top layer of cake in place and cover the top and sides with a thin layer of cream. This is not the final coating but merely a 'glue' to hold the marzipan in place.

Roll out the marzipan into a thin circle, large enough to cover the top and sides of the cake. Remember to roll it out on icing (confectioners') sugar, not flour. Using the rolling pin, drape the marzipan over the cake. Trim any excess; tuck the edges neatly under the cake and smooth over any cracks.

Cut a large cross in the centre and peel back the four triangles of marzipan. You should have sufficient marzipan left to cut away the triangles and replace them with fresh ones. This isn't vital but it saves cleaning off the cream and cake crumbs from the underside of the triangles which are now exposed. Hull the strawberries, cut into quarters if they are large and pile into the centre with the blueberries, or whatever fruits you are using. Put the remainder around the cake. Dust with icing (confectioners') sugar and put into the fridge. The cake is best made an hour or so ahead to allow the filling to soak in. It is fine made a day ahead. Keep in the fridge and ideally remove an hour or so before serving.

Esterházy Torta

This splendid Hungarian cake was named after the equally splendidly-named nineteenth-century diplomat Prince Paul III Anton Esterházy de Galántha. It was invented by Budapest bakers and became popular throughout the Austro-Hungarian Empire. The ingredients can vary, using either almonds or walnuts as the base, more or less chocolate and the addition of cognac, but the essence of the cake remains the same; pure indulgence.

We first discovered it in *Winter Cabin Cooking* by Lizzie Kamenetzky, but after extensive testing amongst the booksellers and estate agents of London (such discerning palates) we have come up with this variation, which earned everyone's approval.

It may look alarmingly complicated but is actually quite simple, as long as you have enough space in your kitchen for 5 layers of cooling meringue.

Serves 12

Meringues
225 g / 8 oz / 2 cups ground roasted hazelnuts
10 egg whites
225 g / 8 oz / 2 cups caster (superfine) sugar
70 g / 2 ½ oz / ⅔ cup plain (all purpose) flour

Filling
120 g / 4 oz ground roasted hazelnuts
10 egg yolks
200 g / 7 oz / ⅞ cup caster (superfine) sugar
250 g / 8 oz / 2 sticks butter, at room temperature
1 teaspoon vanilla extract
15-20 g / ½ oz / 2 ½ tablespoons cocoa

Glaze
2-3 tablespoons apricot jam
1 teaspoon water

Icing
250 g / 8 oz / 1 ¾ cups icing (confectioners') sugar
3 teaspoons lemon juice
hot water, if necessary

Decoration
15 g / 1 ½ oz dark (bittersweet) chocolate
½ teaspoon oil
75 g / 2 ½ oz chopped hazelnuts

To make the meringues:
Cut 5 squares of baking paper and draw a 23 cm / 9 inch circle on each.

You should be able to buy ready-chopped roasted hazelnuts. If not, preheat the oven to 160°C / 325°F / Gas 3. Spread all the hazelnuts onto a baking tray and toast for 5 minutes. Set aside to cool. Divide them into batches for the meringues, filling and decoration. Then grind the nuts for the meringues until they resemble coarse sand. If you are using a processor, do it in short pulses as you do not want them to become oily.

Beat the egg whites with an electric mixer until they form fairly firm peaks, this will take about 6-7 minutes. Gradually add the sugar while beating continuously. Gently fold in the ground hazelnuts and the flour, taking care not to deflate the mixture.

Place the paper onto a flat baking tray and spoon a fifth of the mixture onto the circle. (The easiest way to do this is to weigh your mixing bowl when it is empty, weigh it again when the meringue is ready and divide the difference by five.) Spread it out so it fills the circle and is as smooth as possible. You don't need to pipe the circles; as long as they are roughly flat, the filling will level the cake out. Bake for about 20 minutes. The amount of time it takes will vary according to your oven's proclivities and how many of the meringues you cook at the same time. They should be a rich golden brown and although they will seem soft they should not be sticky. Remove each meringue as it is ready and place it, still on its paper, on an even surface.

Cool the oven tray (this is important) and repeat till all 5 layers are cooked.

To make the filling:
Grind the hazelnuts as before, making them slightly finer.

Fill a saucepan with about 2 cm / 1 inch water and bring to a slow boil. Put the egg yolks, sugar and vanilla extract into a heatproof bowl and place over the simmering water. Using an electric mixer, beat until pale and creamy. Remove from the heat and set aside to cool.

Beat the butter until pale and fluffy. Fold in the egg mixture and add the hazelnuts and cocoa. Mix well but gently.

Set aside 2 heaped tablespoons of the filling to spread around the sides of the cake and divide the rest equally into 4 bowls.

To construct the cake:
Line a flat plate or tray with baking paper. Remove the baking paper from one of the layers and place the meringue disc onto the paper. Spread one quantity of filling evenly over the meringue, then place another layer on top. Repeat, making sure that the last layer is placed bottom-side up which will give you a flat surface for the icing.

Place a sheet of baking paper on the top and press gently to even up the layers. Put another plate or tray on top and weigh down with a couple of cans or a book. Put in the fridge for an hour.

To decorate the cake:

If necessary chop the hazelnuts; we chop them fairly finely but it doesn't really matter, they just need to stick to the filling round the side of the cake.

Put the apricot jam and water into a saucepan and heat gently. Mix well and, if necessary, sieve. Remove the weights, tray and top layer of baking paper from the cake and spread a thin layer of jam over the top disc of meringue.

Place the cake back in the fridge for 20 minutes to allow the jam to cool.

Spread the remaining hazelnut filling round the sides of the cake.

Melt the chocolate and oil in a heatproof bowl or bain-marie over a pan of simmering water. Put into a piping bag or a plastic bag with a tiny hole cut in the corner.

Mix together the icing (confectioners') sugar and lemon juice. Add the hot water a little at a time until the mixture is spreadable but not runny. Pour the icing over the top of the cake and smooth with a large knife dipped in hot water. There will probably be too much icing but you want a fairly thick layer, and any left over will improve any plain cake or biscuit that happens to be close by.

Before the icing sets, pipe 4 concentric circles of chocolate into the top of the cake. Using the tip of a sharp knife or a wooden skewer, run 6 lines from the centre of the cake to the outer edge. In between each line draw another line in the opposite direction in to the centre of the cake, creating a spider's web on the white icing.

Clean off any runs of icing round the sides and press the remaining crushed hazelnuts into the mixture. Return to the fridge to allow the layers to firm up. Ideally remove an hour or so before serving. In the unlikely event of it not all being eaten in one sitting, the cake will keep well in the fridge for four or five days.

Canadian Butter Tartlets

This is another recipe we first discovered in Lizzie Kamenetzky's

Winter Cabin Cooking. A little research revealed that there is no 'definitive' Canadian tart recipe. They were popular with the pioneers and are now eaten throughout the English-speaking provinces of Canada, with each family regarding their version as the correct one. Many purists insist that the filling should simply consist of butter, sugar and eggs, while over the years bakers have added walnuts, raisins, pecans and even chilli, maple bacon and pumpkin. There are now Butter Tart tours, festivals and even competitions. At Ontario's Best Butter Tart Festival in 2014 a staggering 50,000 tarts were sold.

Makes 12

Pastry
200 g / 7 oz / 1 ⅔ cups plain (all purpose flour)
pinch salt
100 g / 3 ½ oz / ⅞ stick cold butter, cut into cubes
2-3 tablespoons cold water

Filling
2 eggs
75 g / 2 ½ oz / ⅓ cup light muscovado sugar
60 ml / 2 fl oz / ¼ cup maple syrup
¾ teaspoon vanilla extract
75 ml / 2 ½ fl oz / ⅓ cup double (heavy) cream
30 g / 1 oz / 2 tablespoons butter
100 g / 3 ½ oz / ⅔ cup pecans, chopped

Put the flour and salt into a food processor and blitz briefly so there are no lumps. Add the butter and blitz until the butter and flour are combined and resemble fine breadcrumbs. With the machine running, add the cold water a spoonful at a time until the mixture just forms a dough. Be careful not to add too much water or over mix. Wrap the dough in clingfilm (saran wrap) and put in the fridge for 30 minutes.

Grease a 12-hole tart tin. On a lightly floured surface roll out the pastry and cut 12 circles 8 cm / 3 inch and line each hole. Save the remaining scraps of pastry for decoration and wrap in clingfilm (saran wrap). Return the tart tin and the spare pastry to the fridge.

Preheat the oven to 190°C / 375°F / Gas 5.

Beat the eggs and set aside about ⅓ to use as a glaze. Beat the remaining eggs with the sugar, syrup, vanilla and cream. Pour into a pan, add the butter and cook over a low heat, stirring all the time (you do not want scrambled egg), until the butter is melted and the mixture thickens and coats the back of a spoon. Remove from the heat.

Stir in the nuts and spoon into the pastry cases. Roll out the remaining pastry and cut decorations for each tart. Simple stars work well, or the initials of your guests; whatever you use, they should be small enough so the nutty filling shows through. Brush the pastry with the remaining beaten egg.

Bake for 16-18 minutes until the filling is just set and the pastry golden. Cool for a few minutes before turning out.

The tarts can be served warm or cold but do need a decent dollop of cream.

Plum and Hazelnut Loaf Cake

This is one of those cakes that can be served for afternoon tea or as a pudding; actually it's great for elevenses too. The cake is very moist, so while cooking, put the cake tin on a baking tray to catch any drips.

120 g / 4 oz hazelnuts
125 g / 4 oz / 1 stick butter
175 g / 6 oz / 1 ¼ cups self-raising flour
pinch of salt
125 g / 4 oz / ⅔ cup caster (superfine) sugar
300 g / 10 oz / 2 cups plums (about 5), stones removed and cut
into small chunks. The plums need to be quite firm
2 large eggs, beaten
demerara (raw) sugar for dusting

Preheat the oven to 180°C / 350°F / Gas 4.

First toast the hazelnuts. Spread the nuts on a baking tray and toast for about 5 minutes. Remove from the oven and, when cooled slightly, rub the nuts in your fingertips to remove any loose skin. Place 6 or so in a blender and pulse to form chunks for decoration on the top of the cake. Blitz the rest of the nuts until they resemble coarse sand.

Grease a rectangular cake tin (23 x 9 cm / 9 x 4 inch) and line the base with baking parchment. A tin with collapsible sides makes it easier to get the cake out.

Put the flour, salt and butter into a food processor and pulse until it looks like fine breadcrumbs. Transfer the flour mixture to a large bowl and add the sugar and hazelnuts. Mix well. Add the plums and stir so they are well coated. Add the eggs and mix everything gently together.

Put the mixture into the tin and bake for about an hour. The cake may take longer to cook; if the top is browning too much, lightly cover it with a piece of tin foil; it should be crisp but not too brown. A skewer should come out clean, but remember it may be wet because of the juice from the plums. As soon as the cake comes out of the oven, scatter the chopped nuts on top, and then sprinkle with demerara (raw) sugar which will melt slightly and hold the nuts in place. Leave to cool in the tin on a wire rack before turning out.

FULLER'S WALNUT CAKE

One of Jane's fondest memories as a child was the treat of Fuller's Walnut Cake. For some reason they were never bought as birthday cakes but appeared out of the blue, usually for no particular reason. They turned up often enough to be dearly loved but never so often as to become commonplace. They were also a treat in Nancy Mitford's *Love in a Cold Climate*: 'Oh Mrs Heathery. You angel on earth, not Fuller's walnut? How can you afford it?' When Charles Ryder in *Brideshead Revisited* goes up to Oxford, he is visited by his stuffy cousin Jasper who 'ate a very heavy meal of honey-buns, anchovy toast and Fuller's walnut cake'.

Fuller's was founded by an American, William Bruce Fuller who opened a shop in Oxford Street, London, selling fudge, peppermint lumps and walnut cake. By the 1950s there were eighty-two shops. At the end of 1968 the company was taken over by Lyons and in 1969 the last Fuller's Walnut Cake rolled off the production line, so to speak. For some reason there has never been a widespread revival. To correct this, here is our version, as best as we can remember.

Cake
250 g / 8 oz / 2 cups plain (all purpose) flour
1 teaspoon baking powder
250 g / 8 oz / 2 sticks butter
250 g / 8 oz / 1 cup caster (superfine) sugar
4 eggs
75 g / 3 oz / ½ cup chopped walnuts

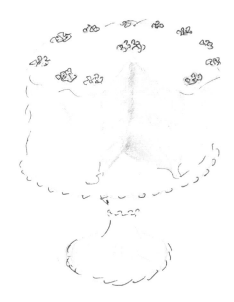

Filling
75 g / 3 oz / ⅔ stick butter, softened
100 g / 3 ½ oz / ¾ cup icing (confectioners') sugar
1 teaspoon milk
½ teaspoon vanilla extract

Icing
22 g / ¾ oz / 2 tablespoons granulated sugar
75 ml / 2 ½ fl oz cold water
1 egg white
7 walnut halves

Preheat your oven to 160°C / 325°F / Gas 3.

Grease two 20 cm / 8 inch loose-bottomed cake tins and line the bottoms with baking paper.

To make the cake: Sift the flour and baking powder. In a separate bowl, cream the butter and sugar until light and beat in the eggs one at a time, adding a little flour after each egg. Fold in the remaining flour and baking powder and the chopped walnuts and gently fold in.

Divide the mixture between the two tins and bake for 30-40 minutes until the top is golden and a skewer comes out cleanly. Leave to cool for 5-10 minutes and then turn out onto a wire rack and remove the paper.

To make the filling: Beat the butter until light and fluffy and then beat in the icing sugar. Add the vanilla extract to taste and sufficient milk so that the filling is fairly soft. Trim the top of one cake and cover with a layer of most of the butter icing. Put the other cake on top and smooth the remainder of the filling to fill the join round the sides.

To make the icing: Beat the egg whites till stiff.

Put the sugar and water into a saucepan and heat till the sugar has dissolved, stirring continuously. Then allow the mixture to boil without stirring until it reaches soft ball consistency (125°C / 240 F). Pour onto the egg whites and whisk until the mixture thickens and starts to hold together.

Spread the icing over the top and sides of the cake. You will need to work quickly as the icing soon develops a crust. Do the top first and put the walnuts in place (one in the centre and 6 round the side if you want to follow tradition). Then cover the sides; you may have some icing left over so try to have some naked cup cakes handy, even we find it is a little sweet to eat straight from the bowl. Then make a cup of coffee and enjoy a trip back to the sixties.

Coffee and Walnut Cake

This is a perfect cake for elevenses or afternoon tea. It is also the ideal cake for a picnic as it is quite robust and travels well. A lot of Jane's recipe tests were sampled by the staff of Hatchards Bookshop in Piccadilly. This cake is one of the ones that made the bicycle journey there perfectly happily.

Cake
220 g / 7 ½ oz / 2 sticks butter
250 g / 8 oz / 2 cups caster (superfine) sugar
4 eggs
250 g / 8 oz / 2 cups self-raising flour, sifted
1 tablespoon instant coffee dissolved in 1 tablespoon boiling water

Icing
125 g / 4 oz / 1 stick butter, softened
350 g / 12 oz / 2 ¾ cups icing (confectioners') sugar
2 teaspoons instant coffee dissolved in 1 tablespoon boiling water
75 g / 2 ½ oz halved walnuts

Preheat the oven to 180°C / 350°F / Gas 4. Grease 2 x 20 cm / 8 inch loose-bottomed cake tins and line the bases with baking parchment.

To make the cake: Put the butter and sugar into a bowl and cream together. Beat in the eggs, one at a time, adding a spoonful of flour after each egg. Then add the coffee and mix well. Gently fold in the flour, being careful not to squash the air out of the mixture.

Divide the mixture between the tins and level out. Bake for about 30-40 minutes until the cakes are well risen and their tops spring back when lightly pressed.

Leave to cool for a few moments and then turn out onto a wire rack and remove the paper. Allow the cakes to cool completely.

To make the icing: Beat the butter and icing (confectioners') sugar until creamy and then mix in the coffee.

Level the top of one cake, if necessary, and spread half the icing onto it. Put the other cake on top and spread the remaining icing evenly over the cake. Decorate with the halved walnuts.

DRINKS AND CONFECTIONS

Maca-a-chino

Maca is a Peruvian root sold in powdered form in health food shops and claims have been made for it reducing menopause symptoms. It has an unusual slightly caramelly flavour and mixed with almond milk makes a beautiful frothy cappuccino-style drink for dairy-free coffee haters.

> *1 cup almond milk*
> *1 tablespoon maca powder*
> *1 teaspoon sugar*

Mix the maca powder and sugar with a couple of tablespoons of milk until you have a paste. Stir into the rest of the milk and froth using a cappuccino machine or wand. Sprinkle with a little grated dairy-free chocolate.

Hazelnut Liqueur

Nut liqueurs: Frangelico, Amaretto and the divine crème de châtaignes are widely available but it is easy and fun to make your own from time to time. As with all flavoured alcohol products you don't need to go mad here and use vintage cognac and bison grass vodka, but equally, the addition of hazelnuts is not going to make that bottle of 50p Bulgarian vodka you brought back from holiday any more palatable; a standard supermarket brand will be fine.

You can reuse the brandy or vodka bottle to store the finished product, but we would advise making this in a wide mouthed jar or bottle as otherwise the nuts will get stuck in the neck and cause infinite frustration.

This is delicious sipped quietly after a meal or mix with soda water or Prosecco for a sparkling cocktail. You can also add to your coffee or drizzle over ice-cream.

150 g / 5 oz / 1 ½ cups hazelnuts, skin-on
250 ml / 8 fl oz / 1 cup vodka
175 ml / 6 fl oz / ¾ cup brandy
60 g / 2 oz / ¼ cup golden caster (superfine) sugar
60 ml / 2 fl oz / ¼ cup water
1 vanilla pod, split

Preheat the oven to 180°C / 350°F / Gas 4. Lay the hazelnuts out on a baking tray (sheet) and toast in the oven for 10 minutes until golden and nutty smelling. Let cool and chop roughly. Place in a wide mouthed bottle or jar with the brandy and vodka. Give a good shake and leave to mature in a cool dark place for two weeks, shaking occasionally.

At the end of two weeks, make a simple sugar syrup by dissolving the sugar in the water over a low heat. Let it cool. Add the sugar syrup and vanilla bean to your nutty alcohol. Leave for 5 days.

Strain the nuts and vanilla bean out of the alcohol mix and discard. Taste and if you prefer it sweeter make up a little more sugar syrup and mix in.

Sticky, sweet and nutty: who doesn't love baklava? The trick to a good one is making it sweet but not cloyingly so and we think we have found a clever cross cultural twist that really delivers the goods. Friends Phil and Gabby arrived to stay via Portugal clasping a bottle of the famous Portuguese digestive Beirão. This is made to a secret recipe so we don't know the exact ingredients (although clearly alcohol features prominently) but a good sniff would suggest orange peel and fennel or aniseed are in there somewhere. After a few glasses we had the inspired thought of adding a little Beirão to the honey syrup on our baklava and 'ta-dah', who would have thought it so delicious? The aniseed and orange cuts though the honey a little to give an exquisite slightly perfumed not too sweet air. If you can't find Beirão (it's available on the internet or make it an excuse for a weekend in Lisbon) then use Cointreau for an orangey touch or just leave the honeyed syrup plain.

You can adapt the nut mix to suit what you have in the cupboard so long as you keep to 500 g / 1 lb total weight. We favour a base of walnuts and almonds with a little pistachio to highlight. Our 300 g filo pastry packets have 12 sheets which need to be folded a bit to fit the pan but the number and size of sheets varies according to brand, so adapt to what you have to hand. You need 4-6 sheet layers each for both the base and the top and a 3 sheet layer for the middle layer.

Makes about 20 pieces

Syrup
250 ml / 8 fl oz / 1 cup honey
190 ml / 6 fl oz / ¾ cup water
100g / 3 ½ oz / ½ cup golden caster (superfine) sugar
1 cinnamon stick
2 tablespoons Beirão

Filling
200 g / 7 oz / 1 ¾ cup blanched almonds
200 g / 7 oz / 1 ¾ cup walnuts
100 g / 3 ½ oz / ⅞ cup shelled pistachios
125 g / 4 oz / ¾ cup caster (superfine) sugar
1 tablespoon ground cinnamon
150 g / 5 oz / 1 ⅓ sticks butter
300g / 10 oz filo pastry

First make the syrup. Combine all the ingredients except the Beirão in a heavy-bottomed pan, bring to the boil and simmer gently for 10 to 15 minutes to thicken slightly. Remove from the heat, take out the cinnamon stick and discard, add the Beirão and set aside to cool.

Preheat your oven to 180°C / 350°F / Gas 4.

Pulse the nuts together with the sugar and cinnamon in a food processor to combine and chop the nuts. Give it a good whizz but don't reduce the nuts to powder; it is nicest with some texture so keep a few nuts in discernible pieces.

Melt the butter in a pan or microwave. Line a 20 x 30 cm (8 x 12 inch) baking pan with baking parchment. Lay one sheet of filo in the base of your baking tray. Brush liberally with melted butter, top with another sheet, brush again with butter and repeat until you have a base layer at least four sheets thick. Cover with half the blitzed nuts. Add another sheet of filo, brush with butter and repeat two to three times for the centre layer. Cover with remaining nuts and then layer up the final 4-6 sheets of filo. Using a very sharp knife cut through the pastry layers to give 20 or so diamond shapes. Brush the top liberally with butter and bake for 25 minutes until golden and crisp.

Remove from the oven, immediately pour over the syrup and leave to cool.

Walnut Whips

Walnut whips were an important part of our childhoods. We have to admit that these, our own little walnut whips are not the same, we think they are better. They are how you might remember walnut whips, the chocolate shell encasing a soft mousse-like filling with a crisp walnut on top, but made with quality ingredients so avoiding that slightly smirched feeling that eating cheap chocolate gives you. They are also a lot smaller, so feel free to eat two or three.

We are evenly split on the milk versus dark chocolate debate. Sally loves dark chocolate, Jane prefers milk. Both are delicious; just follow your chocolaty heart.

Don't even think of trying to pipe the chocolate into that spiral pyramid as you will end up with something that looks like it was left by Fido; buy yourself some of those prettily shaped silicone chocolate moulds. Depending on the size of your moulds you will probably end up with leftover mousse, but it is not really possible to make this successfully in a smaller quantity. Spoon it into a glass and let it set in the fridge, it will make a delicious dessert for the cook.

Makes 32 (depends on the size of your mould, of course; ours are about an 25 mm / 1 inch deep and 20 mm / ¾ inch across)

150 g / 5 oz dark (bittersweet) or good quality milk chocolate
2 eggs, separated
30 g / 1 oz / ⅛ cup brown sugar
125 ml / 4 fl oz / ½ cup maple syrup
½ tablespoon powdered gelatin
175 ml / 6 fl oz / ¾ cup double (heavy) cream
32 walnut halves

Set a large pan of water or the bottom half of a bain-marie on a high heat, bring to the boil and turn off the heat. Immediately place the chocolate, broken into pieces, into the top half of the bain-marie or a heatproof bowl over the water and leave to melt.

Oil the moulds. Take a pastry brush and brush the insides of the moulds liberally with melted chocolate. Place the moulds into the fridge for ten minutes to harden, keeping the chocolate over the water. When the chocolate has hardened, apply a second layer to give a shell which completely coats the inside of the moulds. Pop this back into the fridge while you make the mousse. Keep the remaining chocolate as you will need this for the base.

Beat the egg yolks and sugar until thick and creamy. Add the maple syrup and stir well. Put in a heatproof bowl (or bain-marie) over boiling water and stir well until thick (this may take 10-15 minutes). Remove from the heat and cool.

Whisk the cream to soft peaks. In another bowl whisk the egg whites to stiff peaks. Dissolve the gelatin in 2 tablespoons of warm water. Stir the gelatin into the maple mix. Gently fold in the egg whites and cream. Spoon the mousse into the chocolate shells. Keep this level or just below the top of the cup so you can put the base on later. Pop into the fridge for 10 to 15 minutes to set a little.

Take the chocolate (you may need to place it over boiling water for a few minutes again to melt if it has hardened) and spoon it over the top of the filled cups. If your moulds are shaped so this is the top, you can pop the walnut halves on now and leave to set. If the moulds are so shaped that this is the bottom, just let them set and you will need to stick the walnut on with a dab of melted chocolate once they are turned out. Put into the fridge for a minimum of two hours to set properly – if you can wait, overnight is better.

Turn out of the moulds and add the nuts if you need to. Keep refrigerated and eat within 3 days.

Chocolate Acorns

This totally brilliant idea to make truffles even more beautiful (who would have thought it possible?) came from a Christmas article in *Sainsbury's Magazine*. We used our own fail-safe truffle recipe and chopped hazelnuts but the inspired shape is all theirs. *Matchmakers* are a delicious thin matchstick-shaped chocolate, any similar thin stick of chocolate will work.

Makes about 20 acorns

50 g / 1 ¼ oz / ¼ cup dried cherries, chopped
2 tablespoons kirsch
30 g / 1 oz / 1 ½ tablespoons butter
30 ml / 1 fl oz / 2 tablespoons double (heavy) cream
125 g / 4 oz dark (bittersweet) chocolate
1 small egg yolk
cocoa powder, sifted, to roll
45 g / 1½ oz dark (bittersweet) chocolate for dipping
30 g / 1 oz finely chopped hazelnuts, toasted
5 orange Matchmakers

Put the cherries in the kirsch and leave to soak for at least one hour.

Bring a saucepan of water to the boil and remove from the heat. Put the first measure of chocolate, butter and cream in a heatproof bowl or a bain-marie and place over the hot water and leave to melt.

Stir occasionally, add the egg yolk, fruit and soaking liquor and stir to combine. Put into the fridge and chill until set.

Form into small balls (about a teaspoon size). Dust your hands in cocoa and roll gently into acorn shapes. Dust with more cocoa powder and return to the fridge to chill for half an hour.

Melt the dipping chocolate over hot water as before. Place the chopped hazelnuts on a sheet of greaseproof paper. Using a toothpick spear each acorn and dip the thicker end halfway into the chocolate. Roll in the chopped nuts to coat. Cut the *Matchmakers* into short lengths and press into the thicker dipped end to form a stalk.

GLOSSARY

ACID: soil with a pH of less than 7.

ALKALINE: soil with a pH of more than 7.

ANCIENT WOODLAND: woodland that has been continuously managed since at least 1700 or a wooded site that has had a continuous cover of woodland for over 400 years.

ANTIOXIDANT: a substance such as Vitamin C or E that removes potentially damaging free radicals in the body

ANTHOCYANIDIN; a plant pigment believed to have antioxidant properties

ARGININE: an amino acid present in protein

BARE-ROOTED PLANTS: plants sold during their dormant season without soil around their roots.

BLANK NUT: a term used by Kentish growers to describe an empty hazelnut husk.

CATECHIN: a flavonoid with antioxidant properties

COPPICING: the practice of cutting down young growth to the stool or base of the plant.

COPSE: a small group of trees, from coppice.

CROSS-POLLINATION: the transfer of pollen from one flower to another on a different but compatible plant.

CULTIVAR: this is short for a cultivated variety and refers to a variety within a species cultivated by man. These are frequently (and wrongly) called varieties.

FAMILY: the category of plant classification which includes a group of related genera. It is botanically important but is not usually given on horticultural labels

FLAVONOIDS: antioxidant phytonutrients found in fruits and vegetables

FOLATE: one of the B Vitamins essential for cell growth and reproduction

FOREST: land originally reserved for royal hunting. It will have defined boundaries and some wooded areas.

GENUS (plural genera): the category of plant classification between family and species. It is based on the plant's botanical characteristics and indicated by its first Latin name.

GOOBER PEAS: an American name for peanuts.

GRAFTED PLANT: a plant which consists of a stem (scion) joined to the rootstock of a different but compatible plant. This gives a degree of control over the characteristics of the plant (size, hardiness, flowering and fruiting times) which is not possible with a plant grown from seed.

HARDY: distinction used by the Royal Horticultural Society to indicate a plant's hardiness: frost tender, half hardy, frost hardy and fully hardy.

HEDGE NUT: see Blank nut

HEELED IN: temporarily planted until the plant can be put in its final position.

HOMOCYSTEINE: a naturally occurring amino acid found in blood plasma. High levels of homocysteine are linked to increased risk of heart disease.

HULL, HUSK: the outer casing, containing the shell and nut.

HYBRID: the offspring of plants of two different species or genera.

KERNEL: the inner part of the seed, often referred to as the nut.

LATERAL: side-shoot growing off the main stem.

LAYERING: method of propagation whereby a shoot grows its own root system and can then be cut from the main plant to produce a separate plant.

MAIDEN: a one- or two-year old tree, usually with a single upright stem, also a tree which has not been coppiced or pollarded.

MAST: the fruit of a tree. Most commonly beech but also oak or sweet chestnut.

MONOUNSATURATED FAT: a so called healthy fat abundant in nuts and oils and believed to lower cholesterol.

MULCH: a layer of material placed on top of the soil. Depending what you use it will conserve moisture, suppress weeds and enrich the soil. Garden compost and well-rotted manure will do all three.

NATIVE: a plant which came here naturally i.e. without human influence.

NATURALIZED: An introduced plant which has established itself and now grows naturally. Often called 'escapees'.

NUTTER: anyone who harvests nuts, cobnuts in particular.

NUTTING: collecting nuts, especially hazels.

NUTTERY: a planting or wood of nut trees.

PANNAGE: a traditional right that was granted to the residents of a forest allowing their pigs to forage for acorns.

PEA STICKS: the twiggy parts of coppiced hazel, either the tops or side branches, which will support peas, annuals and perennials as they grow up.

pH: this refers to the acidity or alkalinity of the soil. pH7 is neutral, above is alkaline, below is acid.

PLAT: Kentish term for an orchard of hazels.

POLLARDING: a similar practice to coppicing, the difference being that the trees are cut 2.5-3.6 m / 8-12 feet above ground.

POLYUNSATURATED FAT: essential fatty acids required by the body to function and develop.

PROPAGATING: making new plants from seeds, cuttings, layering or division.

RECOMMENDED DAILY ALLOWANCE (RDA): the amount of a nutrient considered to meet the daily requirements for a healthy individual.

SELF-FERTILE: a plant whose flowers can self-pollinate, i.e. a flower which can be pollinated by its own pollen, or by that from another flower on the same plant.

SPECIES (sp. plural spp.): the category of classification below genus consisting of botanically closely related plants. The species is indicated by the plant's second Latin name.

STOOLING: see Coppicing

STRATIFICATION: some seeds need a period of cold (mimicking winter) before they can germinate. You can either plant the seeds in autumn and leave them outside over winter or keep them in the fridge over winter and plant them out in spring.

SUBSPECIES (subsp. or ssp. plural subspp.): a subdivision of species, this can be further divided into individual varieties (var.)

TANNIN: a bitter-tasting organic substance present in some plants, especially the bark.

TAPROOT: the main root of some plants. They can become large and fleshy with other roots branching off them. Care should be taken not to damage them when transplanting.

'THREE Ds': Dead, diseased and damaged branches

USDA ZONES: United States Department of Agriculture zones which are based on the average annual minimum temperatures and indicate in which areas a plant will thrive.

VARIETY (var.): a smaller group of plants within a species.

LATIN NAMES

Almond, sweet: *Prunus dulcis*

Almond, bitter: *Prunus dulcis* var. *amara*

Beech: *Fagus* spp.

Brazil nut: *Bertholletia excelsa*

Cashew: *Anacadium occidentale*

Chestnut, sweet: *Castanea* spp.

Hazel, cob: *Corylus avellana*

Hazel, filbert: *C. maxima*

Hickory: *Carya* spp.

Hickory, pecan: *C. illinoinensis*

Macadamia: *Macadamia* spp.

Oak: *Quercus* spp.

Peanut: *Arachis hypogaea*

Pistachio: *Pistacia vera*

Walnut: *Juglans* spp.

BIBLIOGRAPHY

THE STORY OF NUTS

Albala, Ken, *Nuts: A Global History,* Reaktion Books, 2014

Campbell-Culver, Maggie, *A Passion for Trees: The Legacy of John Evelyn,* Eden Project Books, 2006

Clifford, Sue and King, Angela for Common Ground, *England in Particular,* Hodder and Stoughton, 2006

Davidson, Alan, *The Oxford Companion to Food,* Oxford University Press, 2014

Flowerdew, Bob, *The Complete Fruit Book,* Kyle Cathie, 1995

Greenoak, Francesca, *Forgotten Fruit,* Andre Deutsch, 1983

Grigson, Geoffrey, *The Englishman's Flora,* Phoenix House, 1958

Hoffmann, E. T. A. *The Nutcracker,* translated by Mrs St. Simon 1853, Hesperus Press Limited, 2014

Howes, F. N. *Nuts: Their Production and Everyday Use,* Faber 1948

Jack, Albert, *Pop Goes the Weasel: The Secret Meanings of Nursery Rhymes,* Allen Lane, 2008

Loohuizen, Ria, *On Chestnuts: The Trees and their Seeds,* Prospect Books, 2006

Mabey, Richard, *Flora Britannica,* Sinclair-Stevenson, 1996

Mabey, Richard, *Beechcombings: The Narrative of Trees,* Chatto and Windus, 2007

McGee, Harold, *McGee on Food and Cooking,* Hodder and Stoughton, 2004

Miles, Archie, *The British Oak,* Constable, 2016

The Oxford Dictionary of Nursery Rhymes, edited by Iona and Peter Opie, OUP, 1997

Roach, F. A. *The Cultivated Fruits of Britain,* Blackwell, 1985

Roberts, Jonathan, *Cabbages and Kings: the Origins of Fruit and Vegetables,* HarperCollins, 2001

Rosengarten, Jr., Frederic, *The Book of Edible Nuts,* Walker and Company, 1984

Thoreau, Henry David, *Wild Fruits,* W. W. Norton and Company, 2000
Uglow, Jenny, *A Little History of British Gardening,* Chatto and Windus, 2004
Willes, Margaret, *Shakespearean Botanical,* Bodleian Library, 2015
Yeatman, Marwood, *The Last Food of England,* Ebury Press, 2007

NUTS FOR HEALTH

Chaplin, Amy, *At Home in the Whole food Kitchen*, Jacqui Small, 2014
Heinerman, John*, Heinerman's Encyclopedia of Nuts, Berries and Seeds,* Reward Books, 1995
Hemsley, Jasmine and Melissa, *Hemsley + Hemsley : The Art of Everyday Eating*, Ebury Press, 2014
Tannenbaum, Cara and Tutunjian, Andrea *In a Nutshell*, Norton, 2014
Wills, Judith, *The Food Bible*, Quadrille, 2007
Wilson, Bee*, First Bite: How We Learn to Eat*, Fourth Estate, 2015

NUTS IN THE WILD

These are a mixture of practical guides and inspiring reads. When foraging in a new area find fellow foragers and ask which local guide books they find best.

Fowler, Alys, *The Thrifty Forager,* Kyle Books, 2011
Irving, Miles, *The Forager Handbook,* Ebury Press, 2009
Lewis–Stempel, John, *Foraging: The Essential Guide to Free Wild Food,* Right Way, 2012
Lewis–Stempel, John, *The Wild Life: A Year of Living on Wild Food,* Black Swan, 2010
Lincoff, Gary, *The Joy of Foraging,* Quarry Books, 2012
Mabey, Richard, *Food for Free: A Guide to the Edible Wild Plants of Britain,* Collins, 1972
Squire, David, *Self-Sufficiency: Foraging,* New Holland Publishers, 2011
Thayer, Samuel, *The Forager's Harvest,* Forager's Harvest Press, 2006
Thoreau, Henry David, *Wild Fruits,* W.W. Norton and Company, 2000

Titchmarsh, Alan, *The Complete Countryman,* BBC Books, 2011

Wright, John, *River Cottage Handbook No.7: Hedgerow,* Bloomsbury, 2010

NUTS IN THE GARDEN

The Royal Horticultural Society A-Z Encyclopedia of Garden Plants, editor-in-chief Christopher Brickell, Dorling Kindersley, 2008

Crawford, Martin, *How to Grow Your Own Nuts,* Green Books 2016

Crawford, Martin, *Trees for Gardens, Orchards and Permaculture,* Permanent Publications, 2015

Hill, Lewis and Perry, Leonard, *The Fruit Gardener's Bible,* Storey Publishing, 2011

Lyle, Susanna, *Ultimate Fruit and Nuts,* Frances Lincoln, 2006

Riotte, Louise, *The Complete Guide to Growing Nuts,* Taylor Publishing Company, 1993

Tankard, Judith and Wood, Martin, *Gertrude Jekyll at Munstead Wood,* Pimpernel Press, 2015

Books by the following on fruit and vegetables are inspiring and informative and often contain useful information about nuts: Common Ground, Mark Diacono, Monty Don, Bob Flowerdew, Alys Fowler, Carol Klein and Alan Titchmarsh.

HISTORICAL COOKERY AND GARDENING BOOKS AND HERBALS

The Roman Cookery of Apicius, translated and Adapted for Modern Kitchens by John Edwards, Rider Books, 1988

Beeton's Book of Household Management, edited by Mrs Isabella Beeton, a facsimile of the first edition of 1861, Southover Press, 1996

Bunyard, Edward A. *The Anatomy of Dessert,* Modern Library, 2006

Culpeper, Nicholas, *The Complete Herbal,* Harvey Sales, 1981

Dumas, Alexandre, *Dumas on Food, Selections from Le Grand Dictionnaire de Cuisine* translated by Jane and Alan Davidson, The Folio Society, 1978

Gerard, John, *Leaves from Gerard's Herball,* arranged by Marcus

Woodward, The Bodley Head, 1943

May, Robert, *The Accomplist Cook, A facsimile of the 1685 edition,* with Foreword, Introduction and Glossary by Alan Davidson, Marcus Bell and Tom Jaine, Prospect Books, 2012

Nott, John, *The Cooks and Confectioners Dictionary: Or, the Accomplish'd Housewives Companion,* Introduction and Glossary by Elizabeth David, Lawrence Rivington, 1980

Pliny the Elder, *Natural History,* translated by John F. Healey, Penguin Books, 1991

Tusser, Thomas, *Five Hundred Points of Good Husbandry,* Oxford University Press, 1984

NUTS IN THE KITCHEN

Books for Cooks Volumes 1-10, Pryor Publications, 2001 onwards

Atherton, Jason, *Maze*, Quadrille, 2010

Culme-Seymour, Tilly, *Island Summers,* Bloomsbury, 2013

Dobson, Ross, *Fired Up: No Nonsense Barbecuing*, Murdoch Books, 2010

Gordon, Peter, *Cook at Home with Peter Gordon*, Hodder and Stoughton, 2009

Henderson, Fergus, *Nose to Tail Eating: a New Kind of British Cooking*, Bloomsbury, 2004

Hollywood, Paul, *How to Bake*, Bloomsbury, 2012

Kamenetzky, Lizzie, *Winter Cabin Cooking,* Ryland Peters and Small, 2015

Ottolenghi, Yotam, *Ottolenghi: The Cookbook,* Ebury Press, 2008

Slater, Nigel, *Tender, Volume II,* Fourth Estate, 2010

Wells, Patricia, *The Provence Cookbook*, HarperCollins, 2004

ACKNOWLEDGEMENTS

We would both like to thank the following:

Everyone at Hatchards and The National Archives for their support of our books.

Catheryn Kilgarriff at Prospect Books who makes writing them a delight.

Teresa Chris, our agent, for all her support.

Jane:

I would also like to thank the following:

Everyone at Hatchards again, this time for their discerning tasting of the recipes and their tolerance of the author in their midst.

Louy Piachaud for her delicious Nut Wellington recipe.

The staff at the library at RHS Wisley. This is a brilliant library with possibly the best setting of any – being situated in a lovely garden and near an excellent café.

Possibly unwittingly, the person who helped me most with this book was Mat Goss. Whilst writing it I was trying to move house; without Mat I would have moved to the wrong place, probably given up trying to sell altogether and certainly not have completed this book. I cannot thank him enough. He and his colleagues were pretty good recipe tasters too.

Sally:

I would also like to thank the following:

Ian Taylor, who is still waiting for a book on meat cookery.

Wendy Hughes, for help with recipe testing.

Paul at P. Cooper and Sons, our favourite Twickenham greengrocer, who found us beautiful nuts when our foraging was less successful than we'd hoped.

Finally, we would like to thank all our friends and family. When we wrote *Berries* they enjoyed, and at times endured, berries with everything. They all adapted brilliantly to a diet of nut-based meals.

INDEX

All recipes are listed alphabetically by the nut under RECIPES. 'History', somewhat inaccurately, includes uses, mythology, old cures and remedies

INDEX Contd.

Nuts